Cultural Differences in Network Communication

Grażyna Piechota

# Cultural Differences in Network Communication

## How Polish, German and Ukrainian Netizens Use Social Media

PETER LANG

**Bibliographic Information published by the Deutsche Nationalbibliothek**
The Deutsche Nationalbibliothek lists this publication in the Deutsche Nationalbibliografie; detailed bibliographic data is available in the internet at http://dnb.d-nb.de.

**Library of Congress Cataloging-in-Publication Data**
A CIP catalog record for this book has been applied for at the Library of Congress

This publication was financially supported
by the Andrzej Frycz Modrzewski Krakow University.

ISSN 2197-1625
ISBN 978-3-631-74862-6 (Print)
E-ISBN 978-3-631-76059-8 (E-PDF)
E-ISBN 978-3-631-76060-4 (EPUB)
E-ISBN 978-3-631-76061-1 (MOBI)
DOI 10.3726/b14333



Peter Lang – Berlin · Bern · Bruxelles · New York ·
Oxford · Warszawa · Wien



This publication has been peer reviewed.

www.peterlang.com

# Contents

# Acknowledgements

The research for this monograph would not have been possible if it had not been for people from universities cooperating at all three stages of research. I would like to thank Dagmar Preiss-Allesch from the Protestant University of Applied Sciences in Berlin and Olga Vygovskaya from the Borys Grinchenko Kyiv University for the organisation and for making this research possible. Special thanks are also owed to all lecturers engaged in the project during my meetings with students and to authorities of each university who allowed me to carry out this research.

Prof. Dr. habil. Magdalena Ratajczak from the University of Wroclaw deserves special thanks for preparing the scientific review and for her remarks that improved the quality of my work.

I would also like to thank all students who agreed to take part in surveys in Berlin, Krakow and Kiev. Thanks to their consent to share their opinions and the will to conscientiously complete their questionnaires, the research project was possible.

# Introduction

Analysing social processes that have taken place on a global scale in recent years, the occurrence of a few global phenomena could be noticed, including increased migrations, conflicts rooted in cultural differences, in particular religious differences, and the rising importance of communication in social media. Contexts of communication processes, including cultural differences, define new challenges in functional analyses. Adopting the cultural paradigm in communication in social media means taking into account the differences that influence the effectiveness of communication and the reception of content transmitted with the use of social websites. According to Gloria Ladson-Billings and Jamel Donnor, in the research of racial issues it is important how you "will be named". Naming someone simultaneously denotes the hierarchy and place in the structures of power. Racial constructs are becoming the determinants of social groups' functioning in contemporary societies affected by the phenomenon of migration, in connection with communication processes that are rooted in cultural differences.

Our consciousness builds identity. Gloria Ladson-Billings and Jamel Donnor believe that we have a multiple consciousness stemming from identity that is changeable and multidimensional, and it is broken by religions, races, sexuality or geographical location of an individual. This influences the shaping of his or her consciousness. Multiple consciousness encompasses the changing identities of an individual, leading to the creation of new political constructs, like "*political race*", which is the modification of the race–power hierarchy and which leads to revitalising democracy, through departing from traditional justifications of an individual's place in the society, and their participation in power as the resultant of the represented race. These new constructs, taking up different forms depending on the country and continent, are usually based on modern civil rights movements, where borders delineated with racial segregation are crossed in favour of agreement and action through culture. A still dominating paradigm of individuals' attitude to social inequality is compassion and appealing to the principle of humanitarianism, which is the major principle governing mobilisation of actions and shaping social relations. However, this paradigm ignores structures that are the source of inequality. In contrast, the construct of "*political race*" rather aims at structural changes (e.g. in education), which make ethnic, racial or cultural differences the source of development and not at replicating the established methods of social hierarchisation [Ladson-Billings, Donnor 2010: 404]. However, this monograph does not concern issues directly connected with race and in this respect is only limited to the theme of shaping individuals' identities and modifications in this area, triggered with social, political and cultural changes. However, this only confirms that the issue of changes occurring in the identity and consciousness of individuals is not only a current matter, but it is also becoming a more and more necessary source of introducing effective social modernisations, reflecting quickly changing reality. Ladson-Billings and Donnor's views on political relativism of race prove that the issue of multinationality and multiculturalism is becoming a more and more important subject of research and postulating structural changes in postmodern societies. The UK's decision to leave the European Union (EU) is on the one hand an appeal to national and cultural identity, which some Britons declared to defend. On the other hand, the action itself seems paradoxical, considering thousands of immigrants living in the UK, also from the EU countries. Moreover, being fully fledged citizens of the country, migrants are allowed to participate in power structures, like the Mayor of London, Sadiq Khan, who is a Muslim originating from Pakistan. This situation confirms existing divisions inside countries.

However, the phenomenon of "*being named*" described by Gloria Ladson-Billings and Jamel Donnor still prevails. It means defining people according to their racial affiliation, regardless of the criteria of equality and social justice. The perspective of perceiving individuals through race is stigmatising for some individuals and limiting for the society in general. "Being named" restricts the description of an individual, ignoring their achievements and position and encapsulating the individual solely in the racial construct [Ladson-Billings, Donnor 2010: 399]. Sylwia Wynter claims that dissimilarities create a favourable perspective enabling people who are excluded from political, economic or social activity to be able to look at reality "at a wide angle", observing the environment from the perspective exceeding the "me/other" notion, not looking for an alternative only in either–or categories and also allowing for other solutions [King 1995: 265–290]. As could be observed, a distinct line dividing individuals into "us" and "terrorists" appeared after the attack on the World Trade Center (WTC) in New York in 2001 in the political rhetoric – a categorisation along the line of racial division or maybe even more of religious division. These divisions in political criteria boil down to creating a political race rooted in the race–power hierarchy. Political race is a construct consisting in creating interracial coalitions and alliances, leading to transformations in forms of participation and to revival of democracy [Ladson-Billings, Donnor 2010: 408–415]. On the other hand, Lani Guinier and Gerald Torres claim that the system creates injustices and political race may be an effective way to expose and destroy preserved hierarchies stemming from racial differences. They emphasise that political race undermines both social and economic racial consequences, departing from traditional understanding of race and the associated prejudices and stereotypes as well as inequalities perceived in the alternative evaluation system "either–or" [Guinier, Torres 2002]. Such a view makes it possible to breach dominating social categorisations that take place in structures, causing social exclusion. Political race appeals to the constant need for social renegotiations, looking for common grounds in the area of identity, national affiliation, citizenship and ethnic homogeneity.

Meanwhile, in Europe there occurs a dynamic renaissance of nationalisms. Political conditions of increasingly anti-immigration climate in the EU countries do not seem unfounded. The situation is similar in the USA, where Donald Trump won the elections using an anti-immigration message in the election campaign and making it an important part of his election programme. Surveys point to higher indicators of crime in districts inhabited by immigrant minorities, terrorist attacks take place, and tabloids explain social mechanisms and phenomena through simple messages, based on stereotypes. The answer to growing fears of people is not a reliable information policy. The source of information is usually mass media, new media and politicians' rhetoric [Zientara 2012].

Migrations are not a phenomenon of the contemporary world (although their present shape is different than the migrations analysed in the historical context), similarly to multiculturalism and development of intercultural communication, which are its consequences. It seems that a considerable group of citizens, mainly from countries that have not long been members of the EU, still lives in an illusion of living in culturally, ethnically and religiously homogenous countries. This creates an impression that problems of the modern world do not concern this part of Europe. However, in Poland there are nowadays about one million Ukrainians who do not only work but also study there, being involved in relations with Poles, tying themselves so closely to the new place that they often decide to stay in Poland. The decision to stay in Poland is also taken by many young Ukrainians studying at Polish universities who are no longer willing to do the so-called 3D jobs (dirty, dangerous, dull), which are usually given to migrants in hosting countries. The illusion of cultural homogeneity is mainly built through messages in mass media and content created in new media. Currently, migrations are not something extraordinary due to the number of people who move but due to participation of the media, including new media, which influences the ways of transmitting information and makes it possible to create virtual groups of people expressing certain attitudes to migrants. Reports in mass media are usually marked with the TV channel's information policy (in public media messages are usually in line with the direction of the policy of the ruling party), and in commercial media they mainly depend on luridness of the message.

Piotr Kraszewski divides migration into emigration, i.e. the perspective of leaving one's country, and immigration, the phenomenon analysed from the perspective of the area migrants head for [Kraszewski 2003: 12–15]. For migrations to take place, two factors are necessary: pushing citizens out of their countries (it may have different sources) and pulling people to another country with the perspective of a better life in the destination country. This monograph refers, in the research process, to both of these definitions of migrations, analysing whether reasons for migration determine attitudes of individuals in the accepting country (or potentially accepting country) and how cultural differences influence attitudes towards migrants.

We divide countries into already multicultural ones and the ones that are becoming multicultural countries. In the case of Poland, multiculturalism is not noticed by the society and by the government. Another division is the one encompassing countries that are proud of their multiculturalism (Canada, Australia) and those that are struggling with problems of the already shaped multiculturalism (France, Belgium). Differences between *countries* given as examples also boil down to the fact that in Canada or Australia multiculturalism has the official status, which is institutionalised and shaped by the state policy. On the other hand, in France and Belgium, multiculturalism has mostly two sources – postcolonial hegemonic policy of countries towards the conquered territories and the effect of the inflow of labour force in the 1960s and 1970s. Both these sources are not the result of implementing a deliberate and planned policy towards migrants but only the result of implemented projects (as ghettoisation of territories for cultivating culture and customs of immigrants, not learning the language by the immigrants or political correctness resulting from unilateral exemption of immigrants from the obligation of recognising these rights that have been culturally inconvenient to them). This led to the situation that instead of creating a harmonious open society striving at common welfare, we have divisions and segregation according to origin or shared values, all the more often identified with religion, causing social conflicts reflected in politics. We may claim that there are countries where there exist parallel societies (notion adopted from Jerzy Nikitorowicz), which exist next to each other, closed in "white" and "coloured" districts, which cultivate traditions and rituals of their own culture, often mutually incomprehensible and unacceptable, what leads to racist, fanatic or even neo-Nazi attitudes (resentment in the lands of the former German Democratic Republic [GDR]). Many countries of the EU currently articulate less or more serious political problems connected with references to the migration policy that the EU is trying to implement. From the point of view of this study, two countries are important – Poland and Germany, where the situation is not the same and each country has its own problems relating to migration.

Poland is a country where after 1945 equality and homogenous national identity was emphasised, which led to the creation of an almost monocultural country, where the administration effectively levelled manifestations of otherness of any kind. After 1989, in a strongly egocentric society, more and more racist or xenophobic incidents have taken place as a response to the changing reality, caused by resentment towards otherness and fear of it. Political parties ruling Poland in recent years have had a distinctly negative attitude towards migration, what is rather the response to social expectations than the effect of a deliberate migration policy, which in fact we do not have in Poland. On the other hand, also the opposition for years has not proposed any solutions that could be treated as a coherent migration policy.

In Germany, on the other hand, with its merger of two societies after the fall of the Berlin Wall, political correctness has dominated, facilitating the creation of multiculturalism, particularly in the western part of the country, where in the 1960s and 1970s thousands of people settled, mainly of Turkish origin. The growth of nationalism and resentment towards foreigners is the effect of events of a few previous years, including the growing number of immigrants who have settled in Germany. Political response to the rise of nationalist movements in Germany is behind the growing importance of the Alternative for Germany (AfD) party. The German society, where integration programmes and multiculturalism policy were introduced in the 1990s, after German reunification, led to the creation of parallel societies[1].

Since the attack on the WTC in 2001, similar events have taken place in European cities (terrorist attacks in Madrid in 2004, in London in 2005 and the events of 2015 and 2016 in France, Belgium and Germany). This led to a situation where more and more often Islam has been populistically equated with Islamist terrorism, activating people against pro-integration actions. Similar politically valid conclusions are made by Charles Taylor while writing about the illusion of equality and the policy of rejection exemplifying "second-class citizenship" [Taylor 1994: 39]. Tariq Modood states that there are certain tendencies concerning multiculturalism. Politicians have announced the end of the concept of multiculturalism (the most spectacular example being Angela Merkel's statement about the failure of the multi-kulti policy in 2010 – author's remark). What's interesting, the failure of multiculturalism in the political sphere has also been predicted by researchers [cit. Joppke 2004; Kundnani 2007; Bagguley, Hussain 2008; Abbas 2011; Husband, Alam 2011]. Public condemnation of multiculturalism intensifies with the terrorist threats or new waves of migrants flooding Europe [Modood 2014: 159].

Changes occurring in the sphere of communication through new technologies create a network society based on certain relationships and dependencies, where individuals enter into relations based on interactions and

1 M. Zawilska-Florczuk, A. Ciechanowicz, Jeden kraj, dwa społeczeństwa? Niemcy 20 lat po zjednoczeniu [One country, two societies? Germany 20 years after reunification], https://www.osw.waw.pl/sites/default/files/prace_35_0.pdf (accessed on 23.05.2017).

using symbols in formulated messages. Contemporary societies are divided, and one of the division criteria is age, determining a certain attitude towards reality. Young people who are mobile, who use new media and enter into interactions with others seem to be more open to phenomena that are connected with the challenges of globalisation, including migrations. Political events of recent years have proven that age is an important criterion also determining the attitude towards immigrants. Age may be the indicator differentiating attitudes of individuals towards immigrants, which includes lower restrictiveness of young people in connection with the presence of "others" in a given country. Such differences of attitudes were noticeable among young people in the UK during the EU membership referendum. The relationship between age and the attitude towards immigrants was also an important criterion during presidential election in the USA in 2016.

In the empirical part (Chapter 4) of this monograph, attempts have been made to find relationships between cultural affiliation of young Internet users and their attitudes and communication behaviour in Internet interactions. An important objective of this study was revealing similarities and differences in network attitudes and communication behaviour in intercultural communication and in relation to cultural differences and migrants. Moreover, the aim of the research was also to reveal the role played by the social media in processes of building tolerance to cultural differences and determining to what extent network communication influences modification of cultural attitudes, thus becoming the reason of a cultural change, manifesting itself in universalisation of attitudes and behaviour of students in network communication. The elaborated methodology (Section 4.1), which describes in detail the three-stage research process, contains questions and hypotheses that have organised the research process, at the same time presenting to readers the intellectual process involved in carrying out the research.

This monograph and research are part of analyses of social change rooted in migrations and the resulting multiculturalism – which is a long-existing phenomenon for representatives of some countries and still treated as a new challenge by others. The context of research was limited to the analysis of the impact of processes of communication in social media in the area of multiculturalism and attitudes towards migrations, including cultural differences.

The monograph consists of two parts divided into four chapters as well as the introduction and the summary. The first part is a theoretical study, while the second part comprises the comparison and analysis of research findings in the field of contemporary intercultural relations on selected examples of communication attitudes and behaviour of young users of social media, representing a high-context and a low-context culture. Chapter 1 contains six sections, where the society in a global sense has been analysed and contemporary migrations as well as their impact on the functioning of nation states have been characterised. The chapter also comprises deliberations over civil society in the era of cultural diversity and the category of multicultural citizenship has been analysed in it. Chapter 2 is divided into seven sections dealing with such issues as cultural identity and its shaping, cultural differences and the meaning of tolerance in contemporary societies. Chapter 3 has been devoted to media and intercultural communication. Like Chapter 2, this chapter also contains seven sections devoted to the analysis of mass and Internet media and intercultural communication. Moreover, barriers in intercultural communication, i.e. stereotypes and prejudices are also briefly described. Another important issue analysed in this chapter is the nature of communication in social media, the role of these media in intercultural communication and promoting tolerance in network communication. Chapter 4, which is empirical in nature, contains results of research carried out in three stages.

The monograph has adopted an interdisciplinary approach to literature, also referring to works from the field of political science, sociology, cultural science and media studies. Literature that was the basis for theoretical considerations comprised studies of Polish scientists dealing with the issues of intercultural relations and the identity of an individual in these relations (e.g. Tadeusz Paleczny and Jerzy Burszta's works), or intercultural communication issues (e.g. studies by Jerzy Mikułowski-Pomorski and Magdalena Ratajczak). In foreign literature, attention should be drawn to Urlich Beck's (and co-authors – author's remark) works concerning the issues of cosmopolitan identity, using the Internet for building intercultural relations and referring to the concept of risk society. Also Manuel Castells' works were used in this monograph, as they are focused on the issues of network communication and building identity in Internet relations. In the theoretical analysis, it was impossible to omit the works of Samuel Huntington, whose "*The Clash of Civilizations*" is currently one of the basic sources for social and political analyses used to comment on rapid changes occurring in the world. Reflecting upon the problems of migrations, the monograph by Castles, de Haas and Miller "*The Age of Migration*" was used, which is a compendium of knowledge about contemporary migrations on a global scale. Finally, Will Kymlicka's studies added thoughts on multicultural citizenship in civil society to this monograph, what must definitely be treated as a challenge of building new social forms in the 21$^{st}$ century.

# 1 State and Society in the Era of Migration

## 1.1 Global Society

Despite the changing reality, many countries still regard themselves as nation states, where the majority imposes a certain organisation of life on others. As Wojciech Burszta rightly notes, long gone are the times described by Ruth Benedict in *Patterns of Culture*, when coherent and closed cultures dominated, that were unaware of the existence of other structures. Today people move a lot, and there are many cultures and different values in the same area [Burszta 2004: 16]. Minorities in democratic structures are guaranteed certain rights and tolerated. An individual is first of all the citizen of a given country and only then a member of a given minority. Basic rights guaranteed to minorities include the principle of equality before the law and civil liberties, giving the individuals the right to formulate and manifest their distinctness. More and more often there appears the notion of the global society, with the assumption that such a society has only the theoretical dimension, and it constitutes an ideological heuristic tool and not a social fact. Lech Zacher claims that lack of referents of the global society justifies its actual non-existence [Zacher 2003: 66–68]. In the theories connected with the shaping of a global society, certain aspects are emphasised, including human rights, non-governmental organisations and other non-state entities functioning globally, sharing common values [Buzan 2004]. On the other hand, Martin Shaw perceives the global society as the exemplification of globalisation processes in economics, communication and culture. He treats the global society as a socially diversified entity, where markets, communication, culture and political modernisation are a diversified area, with many interactions on different levels. For Martin Shaw, the global society is a metasystem which is the resultant of many local, regional or global systems. The values holding the global society together are threats and crises, whereas the issues of safety are the subject of analyses on a local or global scale [Shaw 1994]. In this respect, Shaw's views come close to Ulrich Beck's views about the risk society that are presented in Chapter 2 about shaping individuals' identity. Yet another concept of a global society is presented by Ronald Robertson, pointing to the role of culture in globalisation processes. Emphasising the importance of entities acting globally, e.g. non-governmental organisations that influence the level of individuals' consciousness, Robertson formulated the term *glocalisation*, which is a portmanteau of globalisation and localisation, exemplifying the clash between what is global and what is local.

The problem of a global society is also analysed in its civic aspect. Admittedly, Edmund Wnuk-Lipiński remarked that there is no global civil society but rather some of its institutions have a global dimension [Wnuk-Lipiński 2004: 106]. Samuel Huntington presents an even more radical opinion claiming that it is the clash of civilisations and the cultural differences, including religious ones, that are the main area of confrontation and not creating a common ground of civic participation. But in real terms, the creation and functioning of non-governmental organisations gathering and activating individuals in different cities and also interactions between individuals in the aspect of communication in social media may be treated as the manifestation of bottom-up shaping of civil society on a global scale.

## 1.2 Contemporary Migrations

Theoretical analysis of contemporary migrations takes place in an interdisciplinary context, mainly because migrations have a multi-factor nature, which means that one scientific discipline is not able to explore or fully explain the phenomena connected with it [Romaniszyn 2003]. On the other hand, Dariusz Niedźwiedzki emphasises that this interdisciplinarity is the reason why the analyses are not carried out according to consistent terminologies or methodologies [Niedźwiedzki 2010: 20]. Marek Okólski points to four perspectives of migrations' analysis: influencing demographic changes (fertility and mortality), presenting adaptation abilities of individuals and social groups to changing living conditions, pointing to social mobility and presenting rational behaviour of individuals striving for economic welfare [Okólski 2006: 84]. Zygmunt Bauman calls immigrants people who lose their places, exterritorial entities who rather evoke resentment wherever they go. Both the individuals who are refugees and those who rationally choose striving for a better life are evaluated negatively. Economic immigrants become the symbol of a threat, but in fact the rationale for their actions refers to, what Bauman emphasises, the main virtues that power elites call for in their European voters, including the unemployed – adjusting to the changing conditions on the labour market [Bauman 2003: 282–283]. According to Mamzer, contemporary migrations that take place in the era of integration and going away from isolation of nations are rather treated as a transfer of the individual from one culture to another, where he or she meets different values, norms of behaviour and demeanour [Mamzer 2003: 134].

Stephen Castles and Mark J. Miller believe that people migrate for a variety of reasons. One of the important reasons is economic aspects, that is striving for a better existence, better employment prospects and professional promotion. But the following reasons of migration are becoming more popular: the need to reunite with families whose members have already emigrated, going away from wars and other armed conflicts, the will to marry someone from other cultural circle and striving for a better education [Castles, Miller 2011; Beck, Beck-Gernsheim 2013]. As the authors emphasise, contemporary migrations are the source of certain threats for nation states, which mainly stem from the ability to regulate the flow of people through state borders. Illegal migrations in the 21$^{st}$ century are a global phenomenon on an unprecedented scale. The authors point to tendencies that occur in migration phenomena, which include the following:

1. The *globalization of migration* – migration affects more and more countries, with people from far away places becoming migrants.
2. The *changing direction of dominant migration flows* – Europe has become the major global migration destination alongside the classical immigration countries such as the USA, Canada, Australia and New Zealand.
3. The *differentiation of migration* – migration to certain countries is not of one type, such as labour migration. Migratory chains undergo changes and transformations with the inflow of further waves of migrants, what causes problems in managing social policies both in hosting countries and in countries of origin.
4. The *feminization of labour migration* – the role of women in migration is rising, currently the reason of migration of women is not only reunification of families but also labour migration.
5. The *growing politicization of migration* – migrations are more and more strongly influencing politics in individual countries but they also influence

the shaping of world order making countries look for new security policy solutions together.

6. The *proliferation of migration transition* – traditional lands of emigration become countries of transit migration. [Castles, de Haas, Miller 2014: 16]

Undoubtedly, migrants, regardless of the reason that made them migrate, increase diversity in the society by participation of ethnic groups in social structures of many countries, creating their own associations and participating in cultural, social and economic life of countries and more and more often also influencing political life. Wojciech Łukowski remarks that it is difficult to imagine the contemporary world without mass migration movements, particularly in the context of innovations and development that migrants bring about [Łukowski 2008: 33]. The problem, which in this context – of balancing potential threats and development opportunities – is appearing in connection with migrants, is the implementation of an effective migration policy. Regulation of the flow of migrants, evaluation of the volume of migration (what is currently difficult to do considering its large scale) or attempts to define the period of stay of migrants in a certain country – here, as Łukowski claims, we are dealing with a kind of a game between the market and politics. On the labour market, migrants usually do jobs that require the lowest qualifications (an example may also be Poles emigrating in large numbers after 2004 to Great Britain where only 1% of them did jobs that require high qualifications). This leads to a situation when migrations all the more often do not have the nature of a one-off change of place of residence from the country of origin to the accepting country but the phenomenon encompasses moving between different places many times, which is not difficult within the European Union (EU) [Arango 2010: 97]. Another problematic issue mentioned by Castles and Miller in the context of participation of migrants in the society is the answer to the key question, if immigrants should be included into the society without considering cultural differences or should ethnic groups decide about their distinctness, retaining their distinct cultures, language and religion. The key question is if immigrants should be treated as entities included into the society, integrated with it or treated as collective entities existing within ethnic groups. As Castles and Miller emphasise, the point of departure for formulating answers to the above questions are historical experiences of nation states with internal ethnic minorities and also policy adopted towards citizens of countries colonised in the past. To a great extent, it is this policy that has worked out national models that define the way how ethnic and cultural differences should be treated and also how to perceive immigrants and shape relations with them [Castles, Miller 2011: 300–301].

One of the first national models that emerged after World War II was the assimilation model that was adopted in Germany and other countries accepting *gastarbeiters* (temporary workers entering the labour market in the accepting country). The *gastarbeiter model*, according to Castles and Miller, was a model based on selective exclusion – migrant workers were in the hosting country temporarily and they functioned in some areas of life – on the labour market. Other areas were inaccessible to them. This model devaluated already in the 1970s, when there was an increase in the inflow of migrants from very culturally diversified countries to Europe. In addition, there occurred the process of family reunification, which led to the expansion of new social structures, where migrants were given civil rights, leading to a growing political and economic influence [Portes, Borocz 2010]. Because of social changes, assimilation was replaced with integration rooted in the assumption that adaptation of migrants to new conditions is gradual and requires mutual adjustment. As Castles and Miller emphasise, integration was a slower form of assimilation, leading to cultural absorption of minority groups into the dominant cultural body. The difference between the assimilation and the integration model was that in the integration model temporary distinctiveness stemming from the culture of ethnic groups was allowed. Another national model is the multicultural approach, which assumes that migrants have the right to participate in all areas of life without limitations and also that they are not expected to resign from their own culture, religion or language. Castles and Miller differentiate two variants of a multicultural model. The first one can be found in the USA, where cultural and ethnic diversity is officially recognised, but without state support for ethnic cultures. In the other variant, multiculturalism is becoming part of public policy, where ethnic minorities are guaranteed state support [Castles, Miller 2011: 301–305].

Intensified migration movements simultaneously trigger anti-immigration movements driven mainly by the sense of threat against the national identity of individuals. It is assumed that ethnic homogeneity represents the concept of a nation – the nation shares a common ethnogenesis. One of the important elements of the nation-building process is common culture and sharing values resulting from historical processes. Anti-immigration movements are in fact becoming movements targeted against multiculturalism and glorifying the sense of identity of the individual who is a member of a certain cultural circle. Anti-immigration movements are characterised by politicisation of culture, using it for pointing to higher culture, triggering ethnocentric attitudes and using symbols for building messages integrating individuals around common symbols [Castells 2009; Castles, Miller 2011].

Analysing the results of migrations, researchers point to different aspects of the carried out analyses. The effects may be considered from the political point of view (increased nationalisms, crisis of the nation state but also redefinition of national identity), social point of view (cultural changes leading to cultural diffusion – spatial propagation of elements and symbols of culture as a result of cultural transfer that may lead to the creation or enhancement of cultural pluralism), ethnic point of view (social structure is changing from homogenous to heterogeneous) and eventually also economic point of view (in this case, the effects of migrations are analysed in the light of, e.g., changes in the social capital, taking into account both the accepting country and the country of migrants' origin) [Niedźwiedzki 2010]. As Zygmunt Bauman writes about this phenomenon, "*With the tested ways of acting being no longer available, we seem to be left without a good strategy to handle newcomers*" [Bauman 2006: 131].

Ernest Gellner exploring nationalisms treats them as political principles, according to which political entities should be identical to national entities. Nationalism is both a movement and a sentiment evoking anger or satisfaction, regardless of the rules being followed or not. Nationalism is also a belief where within the same country ethnic and political boundaries should not overlap and ethnic ideology of the group should dominate in a nation state [Gellner 2009]. Burszta emphasises that nationalism is the evidence that nation is an endogamic group, sustained as the myth of origin organising national consciousness. It leads to distrust of anyone who can be attributed foreign features [Burszta 1998:147]. Another social phenomenon that is activated in the face of multiculturalism is racism, which according to Karen O'Reilly is rooted in geneticist's actions, justifying differences between people, categorising them according to biological differences. Currently, simple understanding and justifying racist actions only with biological differences is insufficient – there appears the issue of the so-called new racism, categorising individuals according to ethnic or cultural differences manifesting themselves in participating in minority groups [O'Reilly 2012: 56].

## 1.3 Deconstruction of the Nation State

One of the concepts of the change of identity is proposed by Manuel Castells, by pointing that "*/…/ states are often ruled on behalf of the interests of a minority /…/ Subordinate social groups, and cultural, national, regional minorities, do have access to power at lower levels of the state, in the territories in which they live*" [Castells 2009: 303]. In network society, where diversification and fragmentation of interests progresses, as Castells writes, there occurs reconstruction of identity. Nation states are becoming inert in the face of the number of tasks and problems, what leads to a situation that they hand over some of them to local and regional levels. Power follows the transfer of competencies. Decentralisation of power legitimises new entities, active locally and regionally to represent the interests of members of these communities in the face of solving problems, also global ones.

Already the research carried out in the 1990s quoted by Castells, referring to analyses made by Pippa Noris, proves that only 2% of people in the world describe their own identity as cosmopolitan, 38% treat belonging to a certain nation as the primary source of identity and 47% of respondents point to the local/regional identity as the basic one. In the case of young people who took part in the survey, the percentage of those declaring cosmopolitan identity was 21% and local identity as much as 44%.

As Castells emphasises, deconstruction of a nation state which is the effect of reconstructed identity may lead to taking over the state by another defined and specific identity (ethnic or religious). In this way, fundamentalisms are shaped and they more and more often take the form of religious communities, which in their nature are supranational. The state is becoming increasingly helpless towards fundamentalisms, which become more and more active (Castells includes in them both international terrorist groups and excluded community groups organising suicide attacks), with the only tool being violence, which in the conditions of network communication is of limited importance. On the other hand, the Internet creates different forms of cultural communities based on new cultural codes, which Castells calls *resistance identity*. Such cultural communities become the source of new identities, where the individual does not identify with civil society and state institutions as points of reference. The essence of functioning of a community is the negation of individualism, adopting collective responsibility and taking care of the individual. Groups are closed and the sense of their functioning is the reference to defensive identity [Castells 2009: 73–74]. Jerzy Mikułowski Pomorski remarks that undermining the role of the state means at the same time activation of communities other than the nation and the state. The importance of regionalisms and localisms is growing, and as he emphasises, two homelands compete with each other: the ideological national homeland and the private homeland, based on experiences of local collectivities. If there is conflict of interests, people choose this local collectivity and manifest the importance of local interests [Mikułowski Pomorski 2003: 43].

Zygmunt Bauman, writing about the impact of globalisation on the contemporary state, points out that its role is subject to strict limitations. Like Castells, Bauman also draws his attention to fragmentation, which is the effect of interdependence created by global capital markets and mobility, as the main factors influencing deconstruction of the traditionally understood state [Bauman 2006: 99–101].

Another concept of actual deconstruction of the nation state is presented by Castles and Miller writing that the modern nation state is the combination of national consciousness with democratic principles, which let each individual participate in the public life, including political life, regardless of belonging to an ethnic group or the practiced religion. As the authors emphasise, there is a contradiction between the idea of a nation and the idea of a society. Political sphere is universal, which means departing from cultural differences in favour of participation. At the same time, the citizen status always means functioning in a given nation, with a dominating ethnic group. And this group usually treats minorities with citizen status as entities of a potential nation, which does not yet control a given territory [Castles, Miller 2011: 65]. A similar stance is taken by Sławomir Łodziński who writes that being a citizen is a bond, tying the individual with the state, regardless of the ethnic identity of the individual. Being a citizen is participating in a political and not an ethnic community [Łodziński 2003: 254]. Contradiction between the idea of the nation and the society requires redefinition of the notion of the nation, basing the definition itself on criteria other than a homogenous ethnic identity. Schnapper emphasises that modern states consciously aim at the integration of ethnic groups in the political and cultural space, taking advantage of political, cultural and religious institutions as well as the education process [Schnapper 1991]. At the same time, citizenship has become the appeal criterion, in the sense of protecting an individual's rights by the human rights system on supranational level, creating the concept of supranational citizenship [Łodziński 2003: 266]. Yasemin Soysal pointing to the increasing phenomenon of supranational citizenship emphasises undermining the importance of national citizenship, with an important impact of, e.g., residency or multiple citizenships of an individual [Soysal 1994]. In opposition to the supranational citizenship, there is the model of a multicultural citizenship, which assumes that the state should not be culturally or ethnically neutral. On the contrary, it should protect human rights and delineate the status of national and ethnic minorities. Ethnicity is not only a private sphere of an individual but also the area that should be subject to state protection [Kymlicka 1996: 75 et seq]. Multicultural citizenship should allow retaining diversity with its source in immigrants and it should protect cultural pluralism by protecting cultural identities and creating a platform for their coexistence with the dominant culture [Kymlicka 1998].

One of the challenges of the modern world is preventing the preservation of categorical inequalities that concern systemic differences in the access to benefits, due to, e.g., different nationality, race, ethnic origin or religion [Tilly 2008: 138]. Thus, it seems in the light of the above considerations that the issue of migrations is consistent with deliberations on the deficit of the nation state, what is particularly visible in the context of analyses of national identity of an individual.

## 1.4 Cosmopolitan Europe

Definition of a cosmopolitan Europe was introduced by Ulrich Beck and Edgar Grande. The authors concluded that intellectual elites appealing to national and state values and blaming European institutions for troublesome bureaucracy and for going away from democracy paralyse the development of Europe (understood as the EU). At the time when this study was made, the first effects of such voices are visible – like the referendum in the UK, where the society decided to leave the EU. The Brexit experience has also shown that, under the pretences of cooperation, the EU member states in fact compete with each other. The basic alternative revealed in the language of rivalry is pointing to the EU or nation states.

Cosmopolitan Europe is, according to its creators, a new political project opposing Europe as we know it – neither a state nor a society. The proposal of organising Europe as an efficient political institution entails, according to Beck and Grande, the necessity to elaborate a common narration, to understand conflicting realities as moments of a joint venture of Europeans and, moreover, a new political vision and a new proposal of European integration will be worked out. According to the originators, the last two should stem from European narration [Beck, Grande 2009: 30].

The project of cosmopolitan Europe encompasses a few areas that require definition. First, authors point to an *open political project*, where the identities of Europeans are transformed and there occurs the shift of legitimation from the state to European institutions. As an example they give the European Court of Justice, which under law implements the vision of a cosmopolitan Europe, quite often ruling against nation states.

Second, *Europe self-creates itself*, which should be understood as reference to common principles, accepted and shared by individuals in the whole EU. So far, it is an important problem that is visible particularly now, in the light of the inflow of thousands of immigrants into the EU. And at this point, there appears a question, what values are shared by the EU's inhabitants? And are they rather based on humanitarian values, on the need to help others, stemming from the sense of co-responsibility, or conversely, they appeal to the confrontation of cultures in accordance with Samuel Huntington's concept? The essence of self-formation of Europe, according to the authors of the cosmopolitan concept, is also the capacity for self-criticism and confrontation with the past.

Third, the *project of cosmopolitan Europe is addressed internally and externally*. So far, the focus was mainly on the internal side – on national and supranational institutions. The external side appears mainly in the light of dilemmas that occur in the context of the cultural shape of Europe – whether it should be a project based on Christian or Oriental-Islamic culture.

Fourth, *European integration is understood as a result-oriented process*. Expanding the EU, as a dynamic process, has certain objectives that can be defined with the notion of Europeanisation. Thereby, with progressing Europeanisation, there occurs the export of political, economic and social norms and principles.

Fifth, *Europe is not an institutional form of the EU*. The authors emphasise that from the national point of view it is difficult to perceive Europe as an actually existing being, but rather as a complexity of beings, in some cases competing with each other [Beck, Grande 2009: 32–40]. For Daniele Archibugi, cosmopolitanism is the conjunction of three principles: tolerance, democratic legitimation and effectiveness [Archibugi 2003: 11].

According to Beck and Grande, cosmopolitanism means respect for otherness and creation of new democratic forms of exerting power outside nation states. The authors point out that cosmopolitanism acknowledges dissimilarities while differences are accepted without their hierarchical aspect, others are different but equal, whereas Europe in the cosmopolitan understanding is the Europe of differences [Beck, Grande 2009: 43–45].

From the point of view of the main theme of this study, attention should be paid to authors' views concerning the shaping of the society in cosmopolitan Europe including "aliens". The influences of West and East determine the plane of civilisations' clash, not only in the Huntington's understanding of the "*clash of civilisations*" concept but also within confrontations of citizens of the EU member states. According to the observers analysing the British referendum in mass media, the inflow of immigrants from Central and Eastern Europe to the UK was also one of the reasons the referendum has been won by the supporters of leaving the EU. Growth of nationalist tendencies, often thoughtless and being the answer to populist slogans of political elites, is visible in the whole EU, although with a different strength and against differently defined "aliens". Residents of countries that were members of the EU before its enlargement, like the UK, France, Denmark, Holland, Italy, Greece, Austria or Spain, appealing to national identities direct their antipathy not only to immigrants from the Middle East and Africa but also to representatives of the countries of the Central and Eastern Europe. Moreover, immigrants from the Middle East and Africa mobilise national identities also in such EU countries as Hungary, Slovakia or Poland, with their sources in the fear of "aliens". Beck and Grande propose to guide the process of Europeanisation of the society on the global and not on the national side. After Yasemin Soysal, they point out that nation states create divisions that are archaic to migration processes: "*By holding citizenship in one state (Turkey) while living and enjoying rights and privileges in a different state (Germany), Turkish guestworkers violate the presumed congruence between membership and territory. Another indicator of the fluidity of postnational membership is the increasing acquisitions of dual nationality across Europe*" [Beck, Grande 2009: 212].

The postulated Europeanisation of national societies according to authors should open them to others, make them permeable and lead to a greater understanding, without omitting diversities and limitations.

The construction of a cosmopolitan Europe is also connected with a cosmopolitan identity, defined as the identity where individuals have their own cultural roots but enrich them with values typical of other cultural systems [Nowicki 2001]. Cosmopolitan individuals are predisposed to cultural actions among representatives of other groups. Cosmopolitan identity is sometimes the effect of transnationalism, also called transculturalism. This means that an individual speaks at least two languages and is influenced by bicultural practices and interactions. A cosmopolitan individual functions in cultural diversification, not being a member of a certain national group. This often concerns people who have double citizenship [Niedźwiedzki 2010].

## 1.5 Civil Society and the Challenges of a Multicultural Society

Considerations around the issues connected with the theory of civil society encompass a few important aspects. One of them, which is vital from the point of view of this study, is the effect of still existing divisions in Europe. The countries of the Central and Eastern Europe, until the early 1990s, were members of the former socialist bloc, where structures of the civil society were shaped as the expression of opposition against regimes. On the other hand, in Western Europe the deficit of civil society deepened, which was the effect of globalisation, individualisation processes and questioning of the concept of a welfare state. Changes taking place at the turn of the 20$^{th}$ and 21$^{st}$ century led to the need of restitution of the idea of the civil society, e.g. appealing to the emphasis on pluralism and tolerance as values important for the idea of civil society, based on historical values and experiences. Wioletta Szymczak remarks that the importance of values in the creation of civil society stems from classical theories of civil society – liberal and communitarianist (republican). Each of these theories treats freedom as the superior value, which implicates pluralism understood as a multitude of unitary interests (for communitarians this means decentralised structures, bottom-up activity and a multitude of concepts of good life) as well as autonomy, understood as defining relations between the individual and the community and civic entities and the state [Szymczak 2007: 27]. The quoted author also cites the definition of the civil society put forward by Edward Shils, who presented the relation between autonomy and social pluralism. He claimed that "*civil society is such a pluralist society where the autonomy of constituting individuals, collectivities and layers is limited by individual citizens and groups of citizens' honouring their obligations towards the society as a whole, towards central authorities and laws*" [Szymczak 2007].

Civil society is also manifested in participation and the sense of solidarity. Each of these values is differently interpreted in the above theories. In liberal theory, participation signifies expression of an individual's freedom, which manifests itself in working for a community. In the communitarian theory, participation is a value in itself, with a bonding function, signifying affiliation of individuals in a community with which they share the same culture, identifying their identity. The sense of solidarity in liberal theory is the relation between independent individuals, based on their moral attitudes. In republican theory, however, solidarity is treated as the basic value, independent of individuals.

Regardless of the attributes of the civil society and values that define it depending on the adopted theory of the society's functioning, freedom, pluralism and autonomy are, according to Wioletta Szymczak, the core of the civil society. But its important content is also the ethical aspect that influences the creation of the society through forms of civil activation, the ability to achieve consensus, bottom-up attitudes of citizens externalised in participation, in aid of both attaining certain goals and acting for the benefit of certain groups of people. Edward Balawajder points out that civil society is also characterised by the ability to create values – what is more, values that emerge from the model of civil society are of political nature. They are the effect of accumulation of cultural values, education, which is the resultant of the dominating culture rooted in common beliefs [Balawajder 2007: 77]. Relations existing in modern pluralism, which is one of the main attributes of the post-modern civil society, not only enable the existence of many groups and belonging to those that the individual chooses as attractive but also condemn discrimination, exclusion and paying attention to the deficit of tolerance in social relations.

At the EU level, the significance of the civil society is emphasised as a way to solve new political problems that emerge in connection with the fall of totalitarian regimes, growing phenomenon of mass migration to the EU countries and gradual growth of nationalisms, leading to weakening structures of the EU institutions. The role of the civil society on the EU level is marked as the desired increase in participation, improvement of participation of citizens in decision-making and consultation processes. Another role provided for civil society is monitoring the relations between the public sphere and the private and corporate spheres in the context of pursuing public policies and popularising new principles that aid in solving the emerging problems. Particular importance is given to non-governmental organisations as the exemplification of structural forms of the civil society, at the same time admitting that it is the organisations themselves that are responsible for institutionalisation of social movements and are the answer to the deficit of democracy manifested in the sense of conflict of interests of citizens and elites representing them [Wódz 2007: 12].

## 1.6 Multicultural Citizenship

Considerations connected with multiculturalism in the context of citizenship are the exemplification of diversity in the context of civil society development. As Marta Warat emphasises, contemporary concepts of multicultural citizenship do not concern the process of obtaining or holding citizenship in the legal sense but rather the social and cultural aspect of this phenomenon, which concerns the rights, obligations, participation and the identity of individuals [Warat 2008: 76]. Multicultural citizenship models emphasise the role of culture as a factor defining the group identity of an individual. Both Charles Taylor and Will Kymlicka – authors of the multicultural citizenship concept – remark that every individual is involved in many communities of different nature, from political to social. Membership in these groups defines citizenship in a broader sense than the classically defined citizenship, as the relation of an individual with the state. Referring to the concept of Taylor and Kymlicka, Warat mentions that the essence of a multicultural citizenship is the connection between culture, identity and membership in a certain group and the state, which should guarantee the ideas of equality of all citizens [Warat 2008: 71]. The authors of the above two models of multicultural citizenship emphasise the importance of public institutions as guarantees of the existence of a multicultural citizenship. Charles Taylor points to the necessity of strengthening the non-discrimination policy and promote the policy of equality as the guarantee of the existence of a multicultural citizenship [Taylor 1995]. Will Kymlicka, on the other hand, points to the importance of the cultural dimension of institutions as the guarantee of development of new forms of civil identity, the creation of which is the result of the redefinition of own national or ethnic identities by participants of the public debate [Kymlicka 2003]. Both researchers emphasise that it is important to create and implement anti-discrimination policies that guarantee fighting stereotypes and manifestations of racism.

The issue of shaping multicultural citizenship may also be discussed from the point of view of governance, i.e. public management. According to Kazimiera Wódz and Andrzej Niesporek: "*The European Union in the previous years has particularly cared about the citizens' identifying its activities with peculiar multi-level governance, starting from local through regional to state authorities, and eventually to EU institutions*" [Wódz, Niesporek 2008: 88]. One of the basic principles of the EU is the principle of respecting cultural diversity present in the member states, including both national and ethnic dissimilarities. An organised civil society should safeguard following this principle, with its organisations culturally connected with the community where they are active will be engaged in consultations and the decision-making process within EU structures. According to Kazimiera Wódz and Jacek Wódz, the process of communication carried out by organisations is multidimensional and modified in such a way as to effectively reach out with information and shape civic attitudes in culturally diversified groups. Participatory model of public management uses the multicultural citizenship model to make public authority more effective in cooperation with social partners, thus supporting the model of inclusive democracy. [Wódz, Wódz 2007]

# 2 Multiculturalism and Shaping Individual Identity

## 2.1 Multiculturalism

The definition of multiculturalism takes into account different scientific perspectives – studies on multiculturalism are usually interdisciplinary in nature and they are within the area of interest of sociologists, political scientists, cultural studies scholars and cultural anthropologists. As a civilizational phenomenon, multiculturalism influences political, social and cultural life. Usually it also modifies attitudes of individuals in the economic sphere, particularly in the context of analysing global effects on national markets. Finally, multiculturalism is also becoming the topic of communication processes in social media and information conveyed in mass media. Multiculturalism thus has a multifaceted influence on the life of individuals, especially that, as has been pointed out before, it modifies the identity of individuals, both in the cultural and in the political sense[1]. Defining multiculturalism is acknowledging the phenomenon of co-occurrence at a given area, within one country of one or more groups with separate languages, religions, customs, traditions and systems of social organisation [Paleczny 2005: 148]. Paleczny also defines multiculturalism as the "*system of phenomena encompassing individuals, cultural groups, processes of development and universalisation of identities of these groups, mechanisms of shaping territorial, racial, ethnic, lingual and/or religious ties. /…/ Multiculturalism is the ground, where dominating, ordered patterns of relations between cultural groups are shaped. Structural, ordered networks of intercultural relations take the form of pluralisms*" [2006]. Wojciech Burszta emphasises that multiculturalism is currently first of all the problem of cultural differences in multiethnic countries but also in countries, where religious or sexual minorities exist, expressing ambitions to exist in the space of national culture. Burszta emphasises that "*one of the*

1 Wider analysis of the problem of identity modification in the context of multiculturalism is made by E. Kosowska and A. Kunce in a collective work *Dylematy wielokulturowości* [*The Dilemmas of Multiculturalism*], ed. by W. Kalaga.

*features of the contemporary world is the growing number of multiethnic immigrant states, and thus the overwhelming issue of multiculturalism as a problem of coexistence of different values within one state organism*" [Burszta 1998: 151]. There exist differences between the presence of multiethnic minorities in the space of mainly big cities and the existence of multiculturalism as a set of policies or the way of political organisation of multiethnic populations. Multiculturalism, according to Tariq Modood, is not an abstract ideology but is deeply rooted in social and political reality; it results from the accepted norms shaping relations between citizens, the attitude to fellow citizens and identifying and overcoming obstacles standing in the way of extending the citizenship "crosswise" [Modood 2014].

Peter McLaren identifies four types of multiculturalism: conservative, liberal, left-liberal and critical. Conservative multiculturalism allows cultural diversity, treating it as an addition to own culture. Cultural diversity is already controlled at the stage of the emigration policy. Liberal multiculturalism means apparent equality between racial groups. For this form of multiculturalism to emerge in full, it is necessary to implement structural reforms of state institutions that will ensure the application of equality principles in practice. Another model of multiculturalism is left-liberal, emphasising universal humanism, blurring cultural differences between groups and values represented by them. The last model – critical multiculturalism – rejects pursuit of sameness in favour of emphasising differences. In the cultural policy of critical multiculturalism, diversity is affirmed, which creates the necessity of a polycentric state policy towards groups representing different cultures [McLaren 1994: 455–474].

Multiculturalism understood by Edward Możejko identifies a few influence levels. First, it relates to ethnically and culturally heterogeneous societies. Second, it means the ideal of equality and respect for minorities, both ethnic and cultural. Third, it takes into account the results of scientific research carried out in different fields, modifying curricula on all levels of education. Fourth, it defines the existing political rules, shaping the ideas of equality among people, regardless of their origin, skin colour, race, sex or religion. Edward Możejko points at the same time that each of these levels is simultaneously an individual defining plane of multiculturalism [Możejko 2007: 148]. In order to simplify theoretical considerations of multiculturalism, we may refer to interpretation of this notion made by Andrzej Szahaj, who regards multiculturalism as respect for other cultures, differences and dissimilarities. Achieving objectives in a multicultural society cannot take place with antagonising the society, making oppositions between one group and another or establishing new hierarchies of cultures. Another prerequisite for defining multiculturalism in a moderate way emphasised by Szahaj is resignation from certain beliefs by representatives of social groups with a fundamentalist mindset [Szahaj 2004: 145 et seq]. As Szahaj rightly concludes, multiculturalism is a phenomenon that requires from individuals to move their own tolerance limits, being open to modifications of identity and requiring mutual respect, also from minorities to majority groups. Sometimes, such behaviour is possible, thanks to the processes of negotiating cultural differences in such areas of everyday life as the influence of migrants on eating habits [Brembeck 2008]. According to Waldemar Kuligowski and Adam Pomieciński, alien cultural forms not necessarily today are becoming the tool of cultural domination because they are subject to interpretation and acquisition in accordance with local reception rules. Research confirmed that recipients originating from different cultures perceive messages in accordance with the cultural code known to them [Kuligowski, Pomieciński 2010: 10].

Tadeusz Paleczny perceives multiculturalism in an objective and subjective sense. The objective sense means real existence of many factors that make up cultural diversity. These are, according to Paleczny, less or more clearly distinguished cultural wholes, from tribal ones to civilisations. Cultural elements create a system of interdependencies and co-relations, subcultures and collectivities of different nature, shaping individual identities. On the other hand, the subjective sense depends on the existence of a multitude and diversity of cultural groups, mutually interacting, the effect of which is integration, assimilation and mutual adaptation of individuals participating in a multicultural collectivity. In the subjective sense of multiculturalism, mutual relations that may vary from hostile, through neutral to adaptation and mutual acceptance of individuals are allowed. Multiculturalism understood in the objective sense depends on shaping individual identities, and in the subjective sense, it is the relations between individuals who are members of different cultures that are formed [Paleczny 2007]. As Paleczny points out, currently multiculturalism is an issue that is analysed mainly from the state and national perspective, although these considerations are often local, national, global and, increasingly, civilizational. After all, multiculturalism has different origins, from colonialism and invasions to migrations, the reasons for which are also sometimes different and not always forced. Usually, contact with the other is multidimensional, from a contact identifying national differences to revealing cultural and religious diversities, manifested in behaviour during everyday rituals. Cultural contact that takes place between the representatives of different groups has the nature of a process, which means that there occur changes – individuals have the possibility to meet the representatives of different cultures, they are "exposed" to conduct they do not know or understand. What is more, in the case of cultural contact, often intergenerational experiences are revealed that are supported with ideological messages. Also migrants are subject to cultural contact, who for various reasons undergo the transfer from one culture to another. Often this transfer has the nature of a transition from closed, rather homogeneous cultures to multicultural cultures, where values, races and religious beliefs blend. From this perspective migrants are often forced to reorient their own attitudes. Recognising multiculturalism as sharing common space by groups with different cultural and ethnic affiliations makes it possible to point to different reactions, from rejection, through neutral tolerance, to acceptance of diversity. What's important, rejection may be not only one-sided but also mutual when groups mutually do not accept their otherness (an example may be the regulation forbidding wearing traditional clothes by women practising Islam in France, which is rejected by the Muslim community).

Paleczny points to models of transformation of individual identities under multicultural influence.

1. Monocentric model – occurs in the situation of a clash of a conservatively oriented identity with an innovative identity. In this model, two solutions are possible: traditions are cultivated or there occurs the synthesis of elements of different cultures, as a result of which there emerges a new type of identity. The individual may be closed in traditionalism or adopts new elements, thus shaping universal identity. This model contains the assimilation strategy causing rejection of current identity and assuming the one that stems from the dominating identity of the accepting country (the example may be Poles in Ireland).
2. Cultural identification model – occurs as a result of cultural syncretism. Syncretic identity emerges as a result of connecting elements of

many cultural systems, usually because of opportunism and functional effectiveness (satisfying one's own needs) for the individual existing in a multicultural environment. Syncretic identity locates individuals between one's own and the accepting country's culture (an example may be the representatives of national minorities, e.g. Afro-Brazilians).

3. Universal pluralism model – multicultural orientation depending on opportunism of individuals submitting to assimilation processes. Individuals are open to multiculturalism and otherness, which builds pluralist attitudes. Often such pluralism is the result of mental discomfort that occurs as a result of conflict of values of different coexisting cultures, which leads to shaping an identity joining these elements (the example may be Hong Kong residents).

## 2.2 Tolerance in Intercultural Relations

Tolerance is the prerequisite for building a multicultural civil society. Aleksander Posern-Zieliński claims that tolerance should be treated as the basic directive shaping new patterns of communication of individuals in the conditions of multiculturalism. The principle of tolerance stems from many sources, including cultural relativism, ideological rationale like religion or philosophy, human rights or constitution. An important factor is also social pragmatics, aimed at creating partnership principles of cooperation and cohabitation of individuals in an integrated environment. Tolerance is also an equally important factor for shaping democratic order in civilised societies [Posern-Zieliński 2004: 27–29]. As the author further suggests, tolerance is not unlimited. Many factors influence its limitations, such as the legal system, social norms or the ethical system, assuming that the last one is rather contextual, changing depending on the political, social or cultural situation. As Posern-Zieliński emphasises, tolerance may be considered in accordance with three models: *dominance and subjection*, where the majority tolerates the minority and the latter agrees with their marginalised position, thanks to which they retain the right to cultivate their own culture (diasporas); *horizontal-mosaic system*, where groups share the same territory but there is no subjection between them, tolerance is pragmatic, it serves the purpose of avoiding conflicts, groups do not integrate; and *democratic-integration system*, where people regardless of affiliation in a group have equal rights and obligations, private and public sphere are separated, where communities are created across group divides, avoiding emphasis of differences and using symbols that introduce divisions between groups. The last model is peculiar to these communities that are formed in countries of immigration origin, where tolerance is the end result of negotiations. Will Kymlicka notes that negotiations leading to establishing the limits of tolerance enable integration of groups despite the existing cultural differences. This method of negotiations should be used by states, for which it becomes a requirement to evolve towards multicultural structures. Kymlicka also emphasises that the negotiated tolerance of other cultures supports shaping civil society [Kymlicka 1996]. Posern-Zieliński, on the other hand, observes that the notion of negotiations may take up three forms: *fight with prejudices and stereotypes* – because they are the basic manifestations of intolerance that occur in all social groups at the same time, so it includes both the minority and the majority groups and usually has the nature of intercultural education; *promoting common values* – such that are possible to accept by the representatives of each group and indicate the intention to create a multicultural community, where each group revises their own norms allowing for alternative values to be cultivated; *testing the patience of the other side* – the minority group checks new living environment as regards the possibility to cultivate their own traditions and customs while the majority group tests adaptation abilities of new individuals and their will to concede, trying to limit cultural expression [Posern-Zieliński 2004: 38–39]. Tolerance is manifested in two attitudes: conscious resignation from violence and kindness to people we do not share our views with. Tolerance may have a positive (active) dimension: it depends on the fact that accepting differences is conscious and a negative (passive) dimension, where certain attitudes are voluntarily endured. Positive tolerance stems from human freedom, sense of autonomy – it means accepting otherness and individuality, manifested in choosing values. Negative tolerance is usually demanding in nature, expecting others to give up certain rights or goods; it aids preserving conformist attitudes that kill the spirit of freedom in individuals [Podrez 2004: 23–24]. As Wojciech Burszta writes, current challenges require the "*rule of tolerant thinking*", which means their carrying out through education about differences and promotion of dialogue between individuals. Both these actions should be an element of promoting tolerance in the process of institutional education [Burszta 2004: 22–23]. On the other hand, Francis Fukuyama, pointing to culture as one of the components of the state and its institutional potential, at the same time emphasises that norms and cultural values can only be somewhat modified by education, authority and cultural exchange with other countries. More time is necessary for the changes to cover the whole society. In the short term, cultural values may be changed only at the micro-level – in certain organisations, schools, villages [Fukuyama 2005: 47].

However, it should be distinctly stated that the authors quoted above do not treat cultural patterns as final and unchangeable. Moreover, it is an undisputed fact that education concerning tolerance is necessary, as it enables mutual understanding. The issue that should be emphasised is time necessary for the changes to become more widespread.

## 2.3 Cultural Differences

An attempt at identifying and describing cultural differences was made by Edward T. Hall, taking into consideration the ground of interpersonal communication. Not only as a researcher but also as a teacher and coach of Americans, preparing them for jobs in other cultural conditions, he drew attention to the need of understanding others as social beings, functioning in cultural conditions. As the creator of the model of culture that is simultaneously communication (*culture is communication, and communication is culture*), he accounts for a few types of human activity, reflecting linguistic criteria in cultural research. And thus he distinguished Interaction, Association, Subsistence, Bisexuality, Territoriality, Temporality, Learning, Play, Defence and Exploitation. As the researcher of human behaviour acknowledging in the context of culture that the most important element of culture is the process of communication, he treated language and the conveyed messages as basic. He believes that language shapes thinking but non-verbal communication is also important. Analysing behaviour of individuals, Hall embedded them in intercultural contexts instead of merely analysing their communication processes in their own culture. It was the element differentiating his research from Goffman's, who analysed the processes of communication of individuals, particularly non-verbal, in their own cultures [Goffman 2000]. According to Hall, cultural systems, particularly those that are based on non-verbal communication, are the effects of ethnic origin of the individual, which is justified by the analysis of the so-called *hidden codes*. Moreover, Hall analysed the meaning of context in communication processes, combining social and cultural analyses. Using the cultures of "high" and "low" context, he embedded individuals in certain situations that he analysed treating them as representatives of their own cultures. At the same time, paying attention to "*hidden levels of culture*", he identified the meaning of participation of individuals in social and cultural life of communities where they live.

Hall's findings from the book "*Beyond Culture*" were mainly embedded in the context of communication processes, also including the so-called hidden cultural levels of two countries, exemplifying high-context cultures (Japan) and low-context cultures (USA) [Hall 1984]. Hall's findings became the basis for further research projects, as a result of which it was intended to state what is the essence of cultural differences and how they influence communication processes.

According to Geert Hofstede the differences lie in values; identities are visible but values are not. Studying the importance of cultures in the functioning of structures and institutions, Hofstede emphasises stronger ties with values than with differences in individual identities. He makes divisions of cultures identifying five categories. The first of them is *power distance* manifested in opposing superiors on the one hand and the superiors' decision-making style on the other. *Power distance* means anticipation and acceptance for unequal power distribution manifested by the less influential (i.e. subordinate) members of institutions or organisations. Power distance takes place not only in organisations but also in families. In the family system, in the case of a big distance, parents expect from children unconditional obedience (hierarchy also concerns siblings). Obedience and respecting elders are a value and not independent thinking and behaviour. In response, children get protection and care, which does not end when they become adults. A strong dependence of younger on elders is culturally programmed, combined with expecting help by elders. On the other hand, in the case of a small cultural distance, parents and children are treated as partners. Parents' objective is to make their children independent as soon as possible. A child should be assertive; they should make attempts and learn from their own mistakes. Other than in the case of a high distance, respect and obedience towards elders are not shown, and there is no showing of protection and care. In this cultural model, parents take care of themselves when they are older, they do not count on their children's help. Family relations are also switched to school. In the high distance, respect is shown to a teacher, the student cannot speak without the teacher's consent and they cannot disobey. Parents react if the student disobeys. On the other hand, in low distance, the relations between the teacher and the student are partner-like; students are encouraged to think independently, to ask questions to challenge truths. Teachers do not expect much respect from students; parents rather stand behind the student than a teacher. In countries with a high distance, it also shapes the relations between the state and the citizen. Citizens do not read a lot of press (they trust the press), rarely discuss politics, and the elections are rather won by parties strongly embedded on the right or on the left (weak centre); there is strong polarisation and the need to be dependent and interdependent and also disparity of income – a small group of very rich people and a lot of poor people. In the case of states of a low power distance, it is assumed that politics and religion should be separated, pragmatism is stronger than tradition and striving for lessening social inequalities with political means is reported. Power, money and status usually should not be interconnected – leaders resign from power attributes. In low power distance countries, middle class is strong, press is widely read but trust in media is low. Politics is the subject of discussions but it does not evoke strong emotions.

Another identified division criterion is the individualistic culture index, distinguishing collectivist and individualistic societies (cultures). In a collectivist society, the welfare of the group prevails over the welfare of the individual; the group influences the individual. Collectivism pertains to societies in which people from birth onwards become members of a group – strong and cohesive. The individual is loyal to the group in exchange for protection and care. Collectivist cultures value training, working conditions and taking advantage of the employee's potential, and in students' opinions – obedience, respect for the elderly, for ancestors, financial support for parents, chastity in women and patriotism. Group affiliation is important. Direct confrontation is considered rude, conflicts are avoided. In a collectivist culture, attitudes are based on patterns drawn from general behaviour. Loyalty to the group is a value, there is support in the family, rituals are important as well as taking part in family celebrations. Collectivist cultures are shame cultures – the group is ashamed of what an individual does, sense of responsibility is collective in nature. Misconduct itself is not the source of shame but the fact if others learn about it. In individualistic societies, on the other hand, the welfare of the individual prevails over the welfare of the group. Individualism pertains to societies in which ties between individuals are loose and everyone looks mainly after themselves or their immediate family. Values in an individualist culture include personal time, freedom and challenge. In students' opinions, dominating values are tolerance, solidarity and harmony in relations with others, lack of focus on competition and rivalry, satisfaction with the taken position. Relations with others in individualist societies are voluntary and they are not fostered. Talking things out is a virtue, because it is the evidence of honesty. People going their own way are preferred, in the society help comes mainly from state institutions and not from family. Individualistic culture is the culture of guilt – people infringing upon the rules of society will often feel guilty. Guilt results from one's own conscience and is independent of disclosure of a misdeed. Self-fulfilment of an individual in autonomous conditions is important.

As Hofstede concludes, there is a relation between the categories of collectivism and power distance described above. A high power distance index means a low individualism index and the other way round. In countries where people depend on a group, they also depend on authority and the other way round. Head of the family is thus the authority. At the same time, Hofstede emphasises that in this area there are modifications, the sources of which can be found in economic development, which, treated as a constant variable, leads to a situation where analyses made only in poor countries or only in rich countries make the relation between collectivism and power distance disappear [Hofstede 2007: 97].

Another identified division criterion is the social role of gender. Masculinity as a feature of societies, where social roles are connected with gender, is strictly defined. The man is responsible for financial success; the woman should be modest, sensitive and caring. On the other hand, in the system where femininity dominates, social roles overlap and they are not strictly ascribed to gender. According to Hofstede, with age people are becoming more prosocial, less egocentric, thus also differences between the intensity of masculine features in women and men get smaller [Hofstede 2007: 137]. Social role of gender also creates differences between the ways of resolving conflicts. In "feminine" countries, conflicts are resolved through compromise and negotiations while in "masculine" countries, verbal confrontations happen, and quite often also physical fights. In countries where social roles are strongly connected with gender, striving for achievement and responsibility for the poor is important, whereas in countries where roles overlap, greater attention is paid to welfare and aiding people in need.

The fourth criterion identified by Hofstede is avoiding insecurity. Culture with a high index of avoiding uncertainty does not like ambiguous situations, also in interpersonal relations. This makes it possible to anticipate and avoid ambiguous situations, but often at the same time also leads to risk-taking. In countries with high insecurity avoidance, the need for safety and security strongly dominates over other needs, at the same time justifying the release of aggression and other emotions. Individuals functioning in a culture with a high insecurity avoidance index are raised in strict rules, defining what is allowed and what is prohibited. In a culture with a low insecurity avoidance index, individuals treat insecurity as a natural part of life. Communication is dominated by kindness and avoiding open release of aggression and other emotions. Other than in cultures with a high insecurity avoidance index, children get only general guidelines about what is allowed and what is prohibited.

Another criterion identified by Hofstede is long- versus short-term orientation. In the case of cultures with dominating long-term orientation, features that bring profits in the future are developed – persistence and thrift are valued. In a long-term oriented culture, it is important for the individual to adapt and also adjust their expectations to objectives they want to achieve. It is different in the case of cultures where short-term orientation dominates. Then the virtue is these features that are connected with the past and the present – following tradition and fulfilling social obligations by individuals, resulting from their status. Hofstede emphasises the relationship between the existence of religious fundamentalism and the functioning of individuals in extremely short-term orientation, where decisions are taken on the basis of current events to which the interpretations of holy books are adjusted, which are the source of fundamentalisms [Hofstede 2007: 244].

Studies in the field of cultural differences carried out by Hall and Hofstede are among the most recognised, but they are not the only ones. Another research was also carried out by Shalom Schwartz identifying ten universal types of values that set principles and goals for people in certain cultures (research was conducted in forty-five countries worldwide) [Schwartz, Verkasalo, Antonosky 1997].

*Table 1: Value types according to Schwartz*

| Value type | Defining goals | Representative values |
|---|---|---|
| Power | Social status and prestige, control or dominance over people and resources | Social Power, Wealth, Authority |
| Achievement | Personal success through demonstrating competence according to social standards | Successful, Capable, Ambitious, Influential |
| Hedonism | Pleasure or sensuous gratification for oneself | Pleasure, Enjoying Life |
| Stimulation | Excitement, novelty, and challenge in life | Daring, a Varied Life, an Exciting Life |
| Self-direction | Independent thought and action – choosing, creating, exploring | Creativity, Freedom, Curious, Independent, Choosing own Goals |
| Universalism | Understanding, appreciation, tolerance and protection for the welfare of all people and for nature | Social Justice, a World at Peace, Broadminded, Equality, Wisdom, Unity with Nature, a World of Beauty, Protecting the Environment |
| Security | Safety, harmony and stability of society, of relationships, and of self | Family Security, National Security, Social Order, Reciprocation of Favours, Clean |
| Benevolence | Preserving and enhancing the welfare of those with whom one is in frequent personal contact | Helpful, Forgiving, Responsible, Loyal, Honest |
| Tradition | Respect, commitment and acceptance of the customs and ideas that one's culture or religion provides | Accepting My Portion in Life, Devout, Respect for Tradition, Humble, Moderate |
| Conformity | Restraint of actions, inclinations and impulses likely to upset or harm others and violate social expectations or norms | Obedient, Self-Discipline, Politeness, Honouring Parents and Elders |

Mikułowski Pomorski [2007a: 215].

Schwartz mainly concentrated on the importance of culture in solving problems that are basic for the individual, whereas Hall and Hofstede emphasised the importance of cultural differences in communication processes. Considerations of Hall and Hofstede concerning identification of cultures with indication of differences between them and how these differences influence communication processes were a starting point for further analyses in which authors considered the consequences of cultural differences for international undertakings, negotiating contracts or functioning of international corporations from the point of view of management and business [Gesteland 2000; Hampden-Turner, Trompenaars 2006].

## 2.4 Cultural Differences and Attitudes to Immigrants

Referring to the division of cultures made by Geert Hofstede, we may notice some regularities that result from cultural differences and the attitude of representatives of certain types of cultures to immigrants. As described by Hofstede, in cultures where collectivist tendencies dominate, groups of a certain identity isolate themselves from others, insecurity avoidance is stronger. It makes the representatives of other groups to be perceived in a hostile way. According to Hofstede, breaking cultural divisions is much more difficult in collectivist than in individualistic societies. Simultaneously, he notes that attitude modification is possible. If foreigners appear in a country occasionally, the inhabitants will retain an ethnocentric attitude. But if foreigners' visits become frequent and regular, this attitude may turn into polycentrism, i.e. recognising that there are no universal standards of assessment and that understanding foreigners requires knowledge of their culture [Hofstede 2007: 339–340].

Differences in the perception of immigrants and attitudes to them become noticeable also if cultural differences result from the criterion of social gender roles. In the case of societies where social roles are distinctly ascribed to gender, there dominates the expectation that immigrants will give up their own culture and assimilation will take place. In the case of cultures where the roles overlap, the emphasis is put on integration.

On the other hand, in the case of cultural differences specified with the insecurity avoidance index, differences in attitudes to immigrants are also identified, which have their sources in perceiving otherness. In cultures with high insecurity avoidance, it is assumed that otherness is threatening and dangerous, that aliens should be addressed and treated differently than the representatives of one's own social group. In states where there dominates culture of low insecurity avoidance, otherness raises curiosity and the way of communication is integrating – individuals address the representatives of alien groups in a similar way as other individuals in their own group. There is a strong correlation between the opinion that immigrants should be sent home and a high insecurity level. Racism has a stronger influence in cultures with high insecurity avoidance and dominating masculine values. Nationalism in countries where culture demonstrates a high insecurity avoidance index has an aggressive nature, fundamentalisms (religious, political or ideological) are more common, there occurs xenophobia and a higher level of prejudice against ethnic minorities. On the other hand, in countries with a lower insecurity avoidance index, a higher level of tolerance for ethnic minorities is recorded, attitude to immigrants is positive or neutral, nationalism is rather on the defensive.

Like Hall, Hofstede also emphasises the importance of intercultural communication, starting from the knowledge of foreign languages, which enable contact of representatives of other cultures in the outer cultural layer. The ability to communicate in many languages usually also encompasses more frequent direct contacts with representatives of other cultures. For intercultural communication in a deeper layer – of exchange and confrontation of values – according to Hofstede, the greatest difficulties occur in confrontation of cultures with different indexes defining collectivism and insecurity avoidance. There are two polarised approaches to minority policies – assimilation and integration; in practice they show that adaptation is easier to obtain using the policy of integration than assimilation. Development of the ability to communicate with others takes place in three phases – awareness, knowledge and skills. The starting point is the awareness that people have been programmed and raised in a different way – the knowledge about symbols, heroes, rituals. Lack of understanding and sharing values does not mean that in the intellectual sphere it is not possible to understand differences. Skills are the effect of knowledge and awareness; they provide the ability to recognise and use symbols, rituals, getting satisfaction from being in a new environment and solving complicated situations connected with it. Learning intercultural communication is hampered by egocentrism, low tolerance for insecurity, and also the existing emotional dysfunctions, exhibiting racist or extremist sympathies.

## 2.5 Shaping Individual Attitudes

A developed individual attitude may function on two levels – explicit and implicit. The first one is conscious, openly stated, and on its basis opinions are formulated and values defined. On the other hand, implicit attitudes are uncontrolled, spontaneous and often unconscious in nature. They are automatic, in a situation where there occur circumstances creating the climate for exposing an implicit attitude. Usually this concerns situations, when the explicit attitude of an individual is at odds with cultural values, where the individual shaped their cultural identity. People who openly distance themselves from racism may subconsciously have an implicit negative attitude to others, which triggers the so-called *automatic prejudices*.

According to Aronson, Wilson and Akert, attitudes sometimes change. The source of changes may be the result of social influence, cognitive dissonance or persuasive communication. Social influence means adjusting one's own attitude to others, under the impact of what others say or do. Cognitive dissonance is experienced by individuals in a situation when they say or do something contrary to their opinions or values. Using the mechanism of internal justification, the individual starts to believe in the uttered words, although they are at odds with what he or she really believes in. On the other hand, persuasive messages formulated with the use of mass media and supported by credible people or celebrities encourage to take certain stances on certain issues, even if values coming from the attitude of an individual are at odds with the message. Researchers analysing changes in attitudes as a result of persuasive communication draw attention to central and peripheral ways of persuasion. And thus, the former are based on the logic of the used arguments while the latter result from credibility or attractiveness of the communicating person. For a lasting change of attitude to take place the former are important. According to Aronson, Wilson and Akert, people who change the attitude after a detailed analysis of arguments more often than not retain this attitude for a longer time, behave according to this attitude and oppose counterarguments than people who changed their attitude as a result of peripheral cues [Aronson, Wilson, Akert 2006: 190].

An important element influencing changes of attitudes is also emotions. Arlie Russell Hochschild claims that they are not only action oriented, but also cognition oriented, at the same time exposing emotions as crucial for survival of individuals in group life [Hochschild 2009: 238]. According to Hochschild, emotions signal messages that make cognition possible for individuals. Their use may depend on arousing fear; if fear is moderate and it lets individuals to logically analyse the message, thanks to which they change their attitude. What is important, the message should contain both emotional (fear) and logical arguments that may become the source of change, because they express information how to deal with the situation. Overtly violent messages that could be used in persuasive communication are not effective – individuals are scared by the viewed content, so rather willing to take a defensive attitude than rationally analyse information. Chaiken also writes about heuristic–systematic persuasion model, noting that mental leaps used by us on everyday assessment of reality help change attitudes, using emotions connected with their own moods. A good mood makes positive attitude possible, and the other way round, bad mood triggers a negative attitude [Chaiken 1987].

Types of attitudes stem directly from culture. In low-context cultures, where attention is paid to independence and individualism, logical message is more important, where individualism and self-improvement are emphasised. And in high-context cultures, where the social group the individual inter-depends on is important, emphasis is put on messages, where the connection of the subject with the group and emotional interdependence is marked.

Using emotions in the process of persuasive communication depends on the process of "non-management of feelings", which has recently been strongly emphasised. What is natural and spontaneous is valuable. This is the effect of culturally imposed need to develop in oneself an instrumental attitude to feelings. Emotions are treated spontaneously, praised as a virtue, something rare and valuable. As Hochschild puts it, emotions are currently the most powerful tool used by culture to manage people's actions "*[...] emotion communicates information. It has, as Freud said of anxiety, a 'signal function'. From feeling we discover our own viewpoint on the world. [...] what we think of as intrinsic to feeling or emotion may have always been shaped to social form and put to civic use*" [Hochschild 2009: 18–20]. Emotions are also an important element of building the message using persuasion, which is later shared in mass media and new media as content distribution channels.

## 2.6 Individual's Cultural Identity

Sociological approach to the notion of culture that shapes individual identity has been present for a long time. Clifford Geertz concluded that human nature does not exist independent of nature [Geertz 1973: 46–49]. Cultural perspective of sociological analysis is one of the most basic analyses that are undertaken in sociological research. Usually, this perspective is combined with other fields, like ethnography or cultural anthropology, but also within sociology itself subfields that are connected with studying the influence of mass culture, media or art on cultural change are isolated. As Dariusz Niedźwiedzki emphasises, "*Social identity is one of the key categories of the analysis of social reality. It enables the study of phenomena and processes that take place in it, as well as the occurrence of changes*" [Niedźwiedzki 2010: 133].

Individuals shape their cultural identity as a result of socialisation. According to Barbara Szacka, socialisation is a complex phenomenon, as a result of which we learn social behaviour, becoming representatives of not only a certain culture but also a certain society. In the course of socialisation, we acquire social competences, learn the meaning of symbols and understand language, interpreting non-verbal communication and other's behaviour. We also acquire cultural competences, which define our identity [Szacka 2003: 137–138]. Thanks to the process of socialisation, the individual is subjected to three mechanisms: *reinforcement*, which defines the reward for behaviour that is in line with social expectations (the opposite is punishment for unwanted behaviour); *imitation* of the observed social behaviour; *symbolic message*, which is mainly verbal information from other people, thanks to which an individual knows what is good and what is bad. Birgitta Svensson regards forming cultural identity as a democratic right. She believes that cultural values stem from human rights and citizenship, which create cultural policy, imposing limitations on the possibilities of shaping the identity [Svensson 2008: 199]. According to Svensson, identity is now the key notion describing political and cultural social relations.

Immersion of an individual in their own culture, which is the effect of socialisation, is usually unthinking in nature, leading to automatic use of symbols, rituals and other attributes of culture. Piotr Sztompka points that diversity of cultures is a universal phenomenon, and currently experiencing cultural pluralism is quite common and happens largely through mass media [Sztompka 2007: 230]. In a situation of contact with other cultures, it is either reinforcement of cultural identity of the individual (taking ethnocentric attitude) or a cultural change that may take up the character of a revolution or conversely, evolutionary change of conditions of social life. Ethnocentric attitude, whose idea is to elevate one's own culture over others and to treat it as more valuable than others, additionally leads to evaluation of attitudes and behaviour and also values existing in other cultures from the perspective of the evaluator's culture. As Wojciech Burszta emphasises "*ethnocentrism is measuring somebody else's field with one's own measure*" [Burszta 1998: 13]. Ethnocentrism is the main criterion of self-evaluation of groups; it determines their identification and identity. The essence of ethnocentrism is the division into "us" and "them", sociologically accounting for studies of social groups in a cultural context. The essence of the division resulting from the affiliation of individuals in different groups remains the basic criterion – one's own group and the alien group, which one may encounter analysing the attitude of a collectivity to its own and alien individuals. Own group is perceived as diversified and individualised; actions and behaviours within one's own group are perceived in a rather positive way, which results from proper attitudes of group members; failures are rather explained with external circumstances. In the case of an alien group, its members are rather perceived as a mass collectivity, where attitudes and behaviours of individuals are not individualised. Moreover, successes of the members of the foreign group are usually the result of lucky coincidences and failures, the consequences of individual actions of individuals. In the assessment of the members of the foreign group, individuals often turn to stereotypes as a tool making contact easier. Division into the groups of "ours" and "others" is usually the source of manipulating social attitudes and behaviours, and also a tool of constructing emotional messages.

A culture clash may lead to cultural relativism, where the multitude of cultures is noticed and analysed in the context of their own symbols, senses and values. Cultural relativism may lead to tolerance, i.e. a state where it is either passively allowed that other cultures exist and their right to separateness is retained or active affirmation takes place, which provides positive values (multiculturalism). However, Claude Levi-Strauss claimed that cultural relativism also means questioning values existing in a given culture by allowing what in one's own culture is evaluated as evil [Levi-Strauss 1960: 411–424].

Another extreme current existing in liberal theories is equivalence of all cultures, rejecting evaluative judgements about cultures and their comparisons, as a result of which there occurs hierarchisation of cultures, allowing equal value of each culture. According to Sztompka, the dictionary of proponents of political correctness does not contain the notion of "other", as a word denoting an entity belonging to another culture [Sztompka 2007: 245]. The European Union (EU) adopted the idea of a "Europe of Homelands" – a structure protecting national distinctiveness, other, local cultures, that may potentially be the source of cultural diversity. It is now clear that the assumption made by the EU leads to many problems and racial or ethnic tensions, not only in connection with the inflow of thousands of immigrants to EU countries, but also as a result of changes in social structures that are triggered by advancing internal migration, mainly labour migration, between member states. Changing demographic structures of western European societies, where national cultures are more and more often forced to coexist with cultures of foreign social groups, leads to tensions and changes in the sense of cultural identity of individuals. Samuel Huntington in "*The Clash of Civilizations*" stated that culture and cultural identity define individual identity, shape patterns of cohesion, disintegration and conflict. Politicians of the end of the 20$^{th}$ century, like Vaclav Havel or Jacques Delors, emphasised that cultural factors will be the main source of conflicts in the future. Building a cultural community, which so far has accompanied the idea of integration of EU countries, all the more often is starting to divide countries, and the source of divisions is differences with their origins in culture. The inflow of immigrants has additionally enhanced cultural identities of individuals, which effectively emphasise the affiliation of individuals to their own social group, at the same time being in opposition to others. Appealing to traditions is becoming a certain fundamentalism, described by Anthony Giddens as a tradition under siege. Simultaneously, on a local ground, customs rooted in traditions become habits or relics [Beck, Giddens, Lash 2009: 135–136].

Analysing the sources of individual identity, Ulrich Beck and Edgar Grande point to religion as an increasingly important criterion of shaping identity. Emphasising the diminishing role of nation states, they point out that it is the religion that becomes an important element of creating the sense of belonging. National or ethnic identities still make blending possible, and in the case of religious identities, we are dealing with the phenomenon of exclusion. Religious authority, territorial in nature, is usually opposed to any changes, preserving the identity of individuals [Beck, Grande 2009: 216]. In the case of western European civilisations, a smaller influence of religion on shaping individual identities increased openness and tolerance of others. In the case of the eastern civilisation, religion is an important factor shaping the sense of belonging of individuals at the same time conditioning relations with "aliens" and limiting social change.

Ethnic identity of an individual has been defined as a collective identity of an ethnic group, which is a lasting and isolated collectivity enabling the functioning of individuals using the same language, having their own tradition including religion, kinship, values and ways of satisfying needs. As part of the existence within a collectivity, individuals have the sense of belonging to a group and the sense of cultural distinctiveness [Bokszański 2006: 74–75]. According to Grzegorz Babiński, ethnic identity is identification, being conscious of distinctiveness and the sense of pride, or conversely, it shows the unwillingness to belong. Ethnic identity may be created and developed only on the basis of individual consciousness, without actual group distinctiveness [Babiński 1998: 193]. As emphasised by Zbigniew Bokszański, in contemporary societies, rather not ethnically homogeneous, ethnic identity is the choice of the individual, depending on the situation and pursued goals. The "*strategic choice*", as Bokszański calls it, is rational, and it acknowledges individual identity in actions for the benefit of their interest [Bokszański 2006: 99–100]. The declining importance of ethnic identity versus cultural identity is also the result of the processes of politicisation of culture. This phenomenon occurs in most countries, where the society is multicultural and marked with migration processes. Stephen Castles, Hein de Haas and Mark J. Miller point that ethnic reasons lose their ideological power and practices excluding minorities are concentrated on the issues of cultural differences. It is the cultural differences that are becoming the main ground determining social differences [Castles, de Haas, Miller 2014]. On the other hand, Jerzy Mikułowski Pomorski points to a "*surplus of identity projects*", which he understands as a phenomenon accompanying multiculturalism. He writes that "*cultural association is becoming less and less connected with the tradition of a metropolitan national society*" [Mikułowski Pomorski 2007a: 42]. A similar stance is taken by Tadeusz Paleczny, claiming that "*monocultural identity of individuals is a natural state of the personality of individuals. Duo-culturalism and multiculturalism of attitudes, orientations and personalities is usually an intermediate state, a transition phase on the way to universalisation of identity. A higher grade universal identity, located above narrower identification, with a smaller, more homogeneous tribal, ethnic, national group is more and more popular in post-national societies that are ethnically and racially complex. A homogeneous, monocentric ethnic and national identification is gradually pushed out by identity characterising postmodern societies, integrating different cultural influences in globalisation processes. The situation of growing multiculturalism in most of the contemporary societies, typical for the dimension of group differentiation of most of the contemporary societies, exerts an obvious influence on psychology, identity and personality of individuals. They are not sure anymore of their cultural association and it becomes multiple, polysemic and multi-contextual*" [Paleczny 2008: 42].

Gordon Mathews draws the attention to the role of the market in shaping individual identities, emphasising that the identity, whether national or ethnic, is always connected with a certain place. The identity that is shaped by the market a priori has no connection with a place, it is global. The sense of belonging shaped by the market is different from the cultural identity understood as tied with the state and the territory. Cultural identity in a global understanding is placed on the market; it depends on the information shaped by the cultural supermarket – material and cultural goods and access to them depend mainly on the individual's wealth [Mathews 2000: 24–25]. Cultural identity is the subject of negotiations. According to Mathews, there is a certain conflict around the cultural identity of individuals, where there is a clash between the state and the economic market and globalisation with tribalism in the political sphere [Mathews 2000: 264]. Wolfgang Welsch notices, on the other hand, that culture is not a homogeneous entity connected with a certain ethnic or national group that would establish intercultural boundaries. The concepts of both multiculturalism and interculturalism have become obsolete. Contemporary culture is intermixed and hybridised – cultures are tied together, they are not closed in the boundaries of national cultures but go beyond them and have the ability to adapt to new conditions, where new cultures exist. Migration processes, unlimited communication systems and economic dependencies influence the hybridisation of cultures. At the same time, Welsch emphasises that cultural identity is private (personal) and national identity is civic (legal). He claims that the individual works on their personal identity, where components of different cultural origin are integrated, and the evidence of identity and cultural competence is the individual's ability to cross transcultural borders [Welsch 1998: 195–209].

## 2.7 Globalisation as a Factor Shaping Individual Identity

Human collectivities are becoming more and more linked with a complex network of economic, political, financial or cultural dependencies. Marshall McLuhan creating the notion of a "*global village*" forecasted that mass media will level temporal and spatial barriers, enabling individuals to communicate on a mass scale [McLuhan 2004]. Currently, the notion of a global village is used as regards communication of the network society with the use of the Internet. One of the cultural aspects of processes of social uniformisation is homogenisation manifested in language (currently the *lingua franca* is English) and imitation, leading to a situation that regardless of the place on Earth, individuals consume the same goods. Sztompka, using the notion of "dictatorship of consumption", characterises it as a phenomenon that is the effect of imperialism of mass media (mainly television), as a result of which similar pictures and content are disseminated [Sztompka 2007: 591]. The expansion of American culture, or as Friedman defines it "*globalisation means Americanisation*" as well as the advancing "*American cultural imperialism*" are largely made by global media, which leads to certain social and cultural consequences [Friedman 2006: 515]. One of them is strong resistance of individuals aimed at retaining their own identity (the identity is enhanced in contact with other cultures) concentrating on the critique of massification and uniformisation of cultural messages. On the other hand, however, submitting to global homogenisation leads to the degradation of local cultures [Friedman 2001, 2006]. Castells emphasises that constructing meanings takes place in a cultural context, which is simultaneously global and local in nature. A common feature is creating messages, formatting them and disseminating them with the use of multimedia communication networks. Interpreting the meaning of messages depends on the communication environment where the individual functions [Castells 2013: 410].

Anna Mrozek-Dumanowska on the other hand points out that "*globalisation triggers the explosion of development of local cultures. This creates the need to constantly work out alternative variants of modern development, based on own cultural patterns*" [Mrozek-Dumanowska 2003: 111]. The author describes the processes of self-identification of individuals, also writing about a certain competition of cultures, where individuals fight marginalisation of their own cultures, wanting to retain cultural identity.

The above-mentioned globalisation of locality enables diasporas in different parts of the world keep in touch with each other, regardless of where their members live. Thus being territorially part of one community, thanks to communication processes, it becomes possible to keep and foster own cultural distinctiveness. Friedman states that globalisation of locality also has the face of reversed globalisation. It is the local media that become global, thanks to both Internet and messages important to local diasporas, which generate communication needs, so also put pressure on creating certain quality of messages, retaining local languages. Friedman mentions that in 2006, Google search engine worked in 116 different languages, including a few varieties of Chinese. Flattening of the world, according to Friedman, happens through Internet search engines, thanks to which content concerning local issues is created using local languages.

But looking from the perspective of the influence of globalisation on the identity of individuals, it is difficult not to recall one of the key theories of Samuel Huntington, originating from the mid-1990s. Huntington, observing changes in the world, confirmed that currently the most important thing is cultural identity (resulting from ethnicity, nationality, religion and being part of a certain civilisation), and the resulting cultural similarities and differences are important for the policy of states [Huntington 1996: 544]. And what Huntington points to, politicians may constructively refer to reality, only changing it in a situation when they know and understand cultural processes in the world. The growing importance of non-western economies, whose development is based on a cultural factor, is one of the challenges of contemporary, globalised world. Another is the instability of identities of individuals of the western world, where people more and more often doubt the universality of western culture, as the one which is modern and civilised. This is manifested, on the one hand, in the lack of confidence of individuals in western institutions, values or customs and, on the other hand, in the desire to retain traditional cultures [Huntington 2003: 548].

Ulrich Beck writes about other forms of threats to the identity of individuals, rooted in globalisation processes, mentioning the global community marked by threats. Potential risks, according to Beck, create new interest communities and new types of threat communities. Increasing anxiety and deficit of the sense of security lead to diminishing the differences, and despite the existing conflicts, the emergence of solidary cooperation. This community is formed despite divisions, also cultural and ethnic ones [Beck 2002: 60–65].

# 3 Media and Intercultural Communication

## 3.1 Intercultural Communication – Theoretical Issues

Cultural differences are slowly disappearing in communication behaviours. In high-context cultures, mostly Asian, silence is important as a context for shaping interpersonal relations. Being silent conveys many emotions – like respect or control [Ting-Toomey 1999]. However, social networks break this cultural rule. Young people from Asian cultures remain in constant communication contact through smartphones and social websites, thus breaking the general principle of silence, delineating the context of interpersonal relations.

International communication is the point of departure for considerations over intercultural communication. Currently its exchange ground is the space of the state and not contacts between states. As noticed by Jerzy Mikułowski Pomorski, a homogeneous, cultural model of the nation usually appeals to the past, where there already were aliens but they functioned only in this role, i.e. as "aliens". A contemporary civic society created by individuals belonging to different ethnic, national and cultural groups that strive to retain their distinctiveness aids multiculturalism. And this may be, according to Mikułowski Pomorski, defined on two planes – as the existence of people belonging to different cultures in one society and the process of becoming the participant of many cultures, without giving the leading role to any of them [Mikułowski Pomorski 2007a: 71].

Mikułowski Pomorski determines three types of communication between cultures:

1. Cross-cultural communication – individuals from different groups communicate within one national culture.
2. Intercultural communication – communication with individuals from other cultures or ethnic groups.
3. International communication – communication at the level of countries [Mikułowski Pomorski 2007a: 14].

Marta Ryniejska-Kiełdanowicz proposes a fourth type of intercultural communication – global communication, which consists in exchanging information, values and opinions between groups and institutions in the global arena [Ryniejska-Kiełdanowicz 2011: 24].

Intercultural communication is a process of communication of people representing different cultures. Stella Ting-Toomey emphasises that intercultural communication takes place when our participation in cultural groups influences the process of communication on the conscious or unconscious level. The individual is not always aware of these cultural differences but he or she always needs to know how to communicate effectively [Ting-Toomey 1999: 16]. Some researchers directly identify intercultural communication as communication between people belonging to different cultures [Samovar, Porter 1994; Molenda-Zdziech 2001; Lustig, Koester 2003]. Regarded as a pioneer of research on intercultural communication, Edward T. Hall equated communication with culture, what may be understood as a natural allowing of differences in communication processes of representatives of different cultures [Hall 1984: 15]. Hall also emphasised, besides programming the world through language, the meaning of context, as an element allowing to formulate cultural differences. Determining the typology of high- and low-context cultures, he simultaneously pointed to differences in the communication of individuals – representatives of both types of cultures. The meaning of context in intercultural communication is also emphasised in Magdalena Ratajczak's writing that in the process of communication with representatives of different cultures, besides understanding, also context and knowledge are important [Ratajczak 2004: 14]. The context is created by different circumstances, currently religion is becoming more and more important as a potential communication barrier. This happens due to unlimited mass communication in the space of new media. Huntington wrote about the influence of religion as a source of conflicts on a global scale already in the 1990s, pointing that religion will be the ground for the clash of civilisations. Religion may be the ground of civilizational conflict also on the communication plane. Irony or satire is one of the tools used in European culture, but when religious symbols become objects of irony or satire then the nature of the message becomes iconoclastic, particularly for Muslims[1]. Intercultural communication in the realm of which social,

1 In January 2015, the most radical example of the Muslim response to satirical texts of the French weekly "*Charlie Hebdo*", which regularly publishes materials

promotional or educational campaigns are currently prepared, which are dedicated to individuals from different cultural circles, requires particular sensitivity to these cultural differences. As Anthony Davis emphasises, the fact that individuals belonging to different cultures coexist in the same space does not at all guarantee similarities [Davis 2007: 238].

Coexistence and sharing the same space shapes individuals who are "*internally multicultural*" – able to socialise in different societies, easily adjusting to changing circumstances and locations [Mikułowski Pomorski 2007a: 15]. Tadeusz Paleczny identifies a few barriers that are important for effective intercultural communication. The first one is language, all the more often replaced by *lingua franca*, which currently means communication in English, not always effectively conveying the specific meanings. Another barrier is non-verbal communication, which is complex and devoid of the virtue of universalism. The third barrier is prejudices and stereotypes, which enable people to easily order the world but at the same time block cognitive abilities of individuals, imposing on them certain behavioural frames. The fourth barrier is ethnocentrism, which perceives one's own culture as superior, making communication between individuals difficult or even impossible, usually in connection with stigmatising negative stereotypes. Another barrier is a high uncertainty or stress level triggered by the necessity to enter into relations with representatives of other cultures, not understanding or not being able to interpret the content of the message. The way to "tame" intercultural communication is intensifying contacts with members of other cultural groups, making them personal and less formal. According to Paleczny: "*Intercultural contacts are the effect of functioning of a dynamic psycho-cultural system, where group ideologies and human attitudes are interrelated and overlapped. The processes of cultural universalisation leading to ubiquitous and interactive activity of people from different cultures, favour the appearance of ideologies and attitudes fostering values based on mutual attractiveness, openness and tolerance. In multicultural environments there appears the propensity of its participants to accept cultural otherness*" [Paleczny 2007: 223]. Wiliam B. Gudykunst and Young Y. Kim defined intercultural communication as a transactional, symbolic process

mocking religious symbols and messages based on stereotypes from other media, was the terrorist attack and shooting of a group of journalists and cartoonists.

encompassing the attribution of meanings between people from different cultures [Gudykunst, Young 2003]. Similarly, Richard L. West and Lynn H. Turner stated that intercultural communication includes interactions and events between people from different cultures [West, Turner 2013]. As Beata Boćwińska-Kiluk rightly notes, it follows from these two definitions that intercultural communication is a certain interplay of its actors perceiving each other through differences [Boćwińska-Kiluk 2014: 141]. Boćwińska-Kiluk also emphasises the perception of intercultural communication as a dialogue consisting in confronting different experiences on a national, cultural, group or ethnic level. Groups in which the individual functions shape the dominating cultures, what in fact leads to a different perception of reality by people belonging to different groups. Cultural differences are not a notion referring to superficial issues, they usually encompass rituals, symbols, value systems and hierarchy of needs that have been shaped for generations. Building understanding between others, which is usually the result of sharing the same physical space, according to Boćwińska-Kiluk encompasses shaping the new meaning and integrating individuals under new principles. This is not the effect of intellectual processes but rather an empirical attempt to regulate social relations according to new principles of approving the "other". Identity is created as a product of social environment in the process of communication [Szopski 2005: 27]. Social theories that combine aspects of cultural differences with communication processes emphasise different contexts. Gudykunst's cultural adaptation theory, which uses Berger and Calabrese's uncertainty reduction theory, assumes that people strive to reduce uncertainty in mutual contacts, what is even more important in the case of intercultural communication. According to Gudykunst, the language of interaction is important and whether or not people are members of high- or low-context cultures (anticipation if the interlocutor will apply cultural norms and then anticipation of his or her individual behaviour). Gudykunst's theory enabled the analysis taking into account two factors – uncertainty and anxiety. Intercultural adaptation means that a person does not feel anxiety or uncertainty. Knowing the language and culture of the country an immigrant feels secure, despite being in an alien environment. On the one hand, a low level of anxiety and a high level of uncertainty mean that a person finds it easy to adjust only in an enclave of their own culture, not knowing the culture of the hosting country and usually also the language. On the other hand, a low uncertainty level and a high anxiety level mean that people have a certain knowledge about the culture of the hosting country and they know the language, but they do not share or accept the values. This type of social adaptation is destructive in its nature [Gudykunst, Chua, Gray 1987]. However, Casmir's Third-Culture Building Model assumes the meeting of two or more cultures in mutual relations, without the domination of any culture over the other and without blurring identities. This theory is based on the analysis of interactions – cooperation that is beneficial for all parties. In the "*third culture*" concept, also called the "*third zone*" culture, people start and create interactions without confidence in the obtained results. They are only driven by motivation to start and keep up relations, what with time develops into new forms described as the "*third culture*", being the resultant of contacts of converging cultures [Casmir 1996: 43–44]. In the cultural orientation theory, Kelly and Glenn draw attention to cultural orientation and its cognitive nature. The result is that in different cultures knowledge is structured in different ways and this in turn results in differences in behaviour, also communicational. Cultural orientation theory is concentrated on certain value systems the individuals use, and also it draws from the national culture. This theory results in axioms that are an attempt to understand the aspects of intercultural communication. They were derived by George A. Borden and they include intention to communicate, which defines whether the interlocutors want to participate in the communication process and if there is effective communication, and knowledge of the limits of the communication system – personal, situational and cultural, manifested, e.g. as communication barriers. Knowledge of the limits depends on the knowledge of one's own culture and the other participant's culture. Then Borden enumerates cultural competences, i.e. the ability to read one's own culture and the alien culture by the recipient of the communication. This concerns the ability to read both verbal communication (language) and non-verbal communication – gestures, cultural symbols and understanding value systems of one's own and alien culture, including the system of social inequalities, position of men and women in other cultures, and manifestations of uncertainty that accompany communication processes. Moreover, the understanding of intercultural communication, consisting in getting to know and understanding one's own culture and alien culture. Cultural orientations determine a certain style, what in the case of effective communication should be understood as one's own style and the style resulting from the alien culture. Borden introduced three dimensions of cultural orientation:

- Associative–abstractive, which concerns the way of acquiring and processing information – the associative dimension consists in emotional and subjective drawing of spontaneous experiences from the environment while abstractive influence consists in gathering objective information subordinated to predefined meanings. It is analytical in nature.
- Particularist–universalist, which concerns the ways of understanding the world. People on the universalist level understand the world according to their own conceptual categories, they draw less from their own observations, whereas people ordering the world according to a particularist style do not perceive it in hypothetical categories and rely in their own experiences, direct relations with other people.
- Cognitively closed–cognitively open, which is characterised by the ability to receive information. Closed style means using stereotypes, schemas and ethnocentrism. Open style is characterised by opposite values – openness to novelty, ability to look on others according to their cultural values [Ratajczak 2006: 18–20].

The presented theories concerning intercultural communication are the evidence that this issue is the subject of new analyses rooted in the changing social reality. The above-listed theories take into account how the picture of intercultural communication changes in the context of increasing social diversity.

## 3.2 Barriers to Intercultural Communication – Prejudices and Stereotypes

Prejudices are one of the most common social phenomena. They are analysed in three components – affective, cognitive and behavioural. Prejudices understood as the affective (emotional) component signify hostility or negative attitude to members of a certain social group, what only results from the fact of belonging to this group. Prejudiced individuals do not notice individualism of members of the group they are prejudiced against, they negatively evaluate the group as a whole. The cognitive component creates categorisations and stereotypes. Categorisation ascribes individuals to groups recognised by norms resulting from the dominating culture. A stereotype ascribes the same features to all individuals in a given group, without noticing differences between them. Stereotypes are not easily changed; they do not always need to be the source of harm, they mainly enable simplification of the picture of the world[2]. The third component, behavioural, means taking active measures towards people who belong to social groups, the individual is prejudiced against. Discrimination as an unjustified or harmful behaviour towards people belonging to certain social groups is, unlike other components, an actual activity.

Jan Berting and Christianne Villain-Gandossi described functions of national stereotypes as follows:

1. They provide common reference systems for members of certain social groups.
2. They strengthen collective bonds.
3. They express common values.
4. They allow discrimination of representatives of other groups if they are considered a menace to "our" values.
5. They emphasise the distinctness of the group and provide opportunities for the demonstration of loyalty to one's own group.
6. They look for a scapegoat in times of crisis [Berting, Villain-Gandossi 1995: 23].

The source of prejudice is culture, which deliberately or unintentionally builds negative perception of individuals different from one's own social group. An important source of creating and teaching prejudice is family, where, as already mentioned, the first socialisation process takes place (primary socialisation). Attitudes acquired as a result of primary socialisation may change as a result of secondary socialisation taking place outside the family; the individual acquires different competences that he or she confronts with the ones they already possess. But the confrontation can only

2 According to Gordon Allport, stereotypes make it possible to use brief information to understand the complex world. People want to do it with the least possible effort because the world is too complex to work out individual attitudes.

take place if the individual finds themselves in a more diversified environment, where they have the opportunity to get to know and understand other values. Agnieszka Trąbka writes about the significance of living in a diversified society and its potential consequences for the individual, reporting on her research on reconstructing identity in the so-called *third culture kids* or global nomads, in which she analysed their attitude to cultural differences. She proved that such people have high cultural and communication competences. This is the effect of their mobile childhood and contacts with representatives of different cultures, as a result of which a child learns foreign languages and acquires such features as bravery, open-mindedness and curiosity, which combined make nomads quickly try to communicate with representatives of other cultures although they do not know certain languages. What's important, Trąbka emphasises that contemporary nomads do not limit themselves only to social contacts, but they also try to use their competencies in other situations, e.g. at work, what enables quick adaptation to new conditions [Trąbka 2014: 125].

Aronson, Wilson and Akert emphasise that stereotypes reflect cultural beliefs – in a given society they constitute easily recognisable descriptions of members of certain groups [Aronson, Wilson, Akert 2006]. As they further claim, research carried out for a period of over 30 years in Princeton revealed that students perfectly well knew stereotypes about certain ethnic and national groups, even in situations where they did not know a lot about the groups themselves. On the other hand, research carried out in the 1990s revealed that students were increasingly unwilling to admit conscious stereotypes, regardless of whether they believed in them or not. Interestingly, such conscious stereotypes were easy to trigger even if an individual declared that they did not believe in them. Stereotypes were triggered automatically, beyond control. But in societies where using stereotypes is politically incorrect, reasoning imposes overcoming automatic reactions, what is not at all the same as when the individual sheds prejudice and stereotypical thinking. Rather they less often outwardly communicate them. This phenomenon is sometimes called *contemporary racism* [Aronson, Wilson, Akert 2006: 362–376].

The threat of stereotypes concerns each social group. Concern that stereotypical expectations will be culturally confirmed in the behaviour of individuals belonging to another social group than the evaluating one is normal. When members of social groups alien to the individual act according to the individual's expectations, the stereotype is not only confirmed but often also enhanced. Stereotypes lead to prejudices and these to discrimination. A manifestation of discrimination is lack of empathy, which leads to a situation that victims of actions, behaviour or attitudes may be regarded as guilty of how others treat them.

An identified source of prejudice is also the phenomenon of national megalomania, resulting from ethnocentrism. The belief that one's own nation is extraordinary, as Jan Stanisław Bystroń claimed, is the result of the conviction that the nation takes up a central place in the world and is associated with higher relations with God, originality of the language, legitimacy of customs and physical normalcy. National megalomania is an issue of attitude to the world; it is the effect of regarding one's own civilisation as the highest one and self-reliant, not having to take into consideration other points of view. An important source of shaping attitudes to the world, resulting from national megalomania, is national literature with its content that is easy to accept by readers and at the same time nationalist in nature [Bystroń 1995: 13].

Another important source of prejudice and discrimination is rivalry over goods and resources, understood mainly in economic and social categories. Already in the 1930s, John Dollard proved the relationship between discrimination and economic competition. He pointed that with limited resources, the members of one's own group who feel threatened by members of another group trigger prejudices and discrimination processes for fear of availability of scarce resources. These prejudices do not even stop to work in a situation when contact between groups does not concern these goods, access to which had triggered prejudice and discrimination in the first place [Aronson, Wilson, Akert 2006: 372].

An important limitation in effective fight with prejudice and as a consequence also with discrimination is their institutionalisation. This means that on the one hand culture shapes certain attitudes and norms of behaviour, but on the other hand such actions and conformity to norms are permitted. The already mentioned *contemporary racism*, which is manifested in political correctness to representatives of other social groups, with simultaneously hidden stereotypical thinking triggers the phenomenon of rejecting immigrants in a less open but more socially acceptable way. This means that such people would not be prone to actively support sending immigrants back to their countries, but they also did not in any way intend to influence improved relations with immigrants or extend their civil rights [Pettigrew 1998].

Fighting prejudice is not effective if it uses education understood as dealing with facts and logic. The source of stereotypes and prejudices that lead to discrimination is usually cognitive bias and emotions, and they do not cause a quick change of attitudes. An effective way to fight prejudice are contacts with representatives of an alien group and staying with them, but under the condition that both groups have the same position (equal status) and common goals [Allport 1954]. Overcoming stereotypes and prejudices is also enhanced by informal communication, interactions with many members of an alien group and following equality norms that have a social nature [Aronson, Wilson, Akert 2006: 378–380].

## 3.3 Functions and Impact of Mass Media in Intercultural Communication

According to Harold D. Lasswell, the functions of mass media may be considered in the light of their input into social development. Lasswell distinguished a few functions of mass media: observation of the surroundings (media serve the purpose of conveying information about the changing world), reaction to the surroundings (providing patterns of actions and behaviour), transmission of historical and cultural heritage (enhancing individual identity, promoting cultural patterns) [Mrozowski 2001: 113]. On the other hand, Anna Kozłowska, quoting the typology of mass media functions proposed by Wright, points that mass media serve an informative, interpretive and socialising function. The first one concerns gathering and transmitting information. The second interprets reality leading to the individuals' taking certain actions. The third enables passing on values and social norms as part of socialisation processes [Kozłowska 2006: 76]. Interpretive function of mass media, according to Anna Kozłowska, is one of their main goals. News transmitted by mass media do not present facts about the world but rather create them. The recipient's task is to put the obtained information in a context that they are aware of and that they understand. Kozłowska writes: "*Reading a newspaper or watching a TV program the recipient all the time creates certain hypotheses about the current message that are immediately tested and confirmed or rejected. Thanks to this process the meaning of news is constructed gradually, it is subject to interpretations and contains each motive or event in its narrative part. /.../ As a result of the existence of these interpretative schemas, certain parts of reality gain special importance while others are marginalised or simply ignored*" [2006: 80]. Interpretation of facts excludes objectivity, because they no longer reflect reality but interpret it. Competences of recipients and structured interpretative schemas possessed by an individual are the main determinants influencing reception of messages.

The analysis of both the function of mass media and its impact on the environment makes it possible to state that mass media are rather concentrated on providing information that culturally and identity-wise supports the social group dominating at a given territory. Moreover, mass media support political actions defined in the historical and cultural context. As Andreas Dörner emphasises, discourse in mass media supports and maintains the existing cultural *status quo* through meeting the expectations of recipients, presenting such content that is in line with the thought schemas. In this way media influence maintaining cultural–social memory and enhance dominating cultural patterns at a given territory [Dörner 2006: 4].

Mass media refer to reality depending on the convention and the tackled issue. The ones that may be treated as objective enable the recipient to shape their own point of view on the presented issue, others provide ready answers based on the persuasive message. The recipient receiving information through mass media is not a passive party in this situation. It is true that they do not have any impact on the content and nature of the message, but the communication act itself triggers in the recipient a certain activity and delayed consequences. Indirect communication that takes place when using the mass media providing not only interpreted facts but also their context is usually the source of certain attitudes of recipients in the future. On the other hand, James S. Rosenau claimed that the behaviour of individuals or groups modifies the behaviour of other individuals or groups. This phenomenon was defined as social influence [Rosenau 1969: 10]. Similar claim was made by Stephen W. King, who believed that the behaviour of individuals or groups of people prompts other individuals to change their attitudes or triggers a change that is the result of other people's behaviour [King 1975: 6]. Social influence on recipients' attitudes through information provided by mass media, according to King, is based on informational and normative influence. The former is modelled on the behaviour of other people – the individual adjusts to the circumstances, regardless of his or her intentions. The latter, on the other hand, means opportunism of the individual treating the behaviour of other people as a pattern for their own behaviour in order to achieve the intended objective [Rajczyk 2016: 35].

The agenda-setting theory, the basis of which was created in the 1970s by Max McCombs and Donald Show, stipulates that mass media not only decide about transmitting certain information but also influence the salience of topics. Mass media create a hierarchical information structure that citizens get and this structure does not depend on objective criteria but on priorities adopted in a given newsroom. The selection of facts that will make the news depends on the broadcaster who shapes the information flow, simultaneously controlling it (control of the news covered and control of topics' saliency). Thus, to a certain extent also the image of reality is controlled, which through mass media is constructed in the recipient. Issues that have the chance to make the news, as understood by the agenda-setting theory, should meet the following criteria: be unequivocal and transparent, surprising, up to date and intensively appealing to emotions (explicitness exceeding social norms), important to the recipient and personalised, i.e. the ones that may be attributed to the activities of certain individuals or groups. It is also important for the selection of issues and giving priority to them if the issues present positive or negative events. Those with a negative overtone are much more salient and more frequently covered because they are deemed important for recipients. Selection of issues also takes place taking into consideration the priorities of the journalists themselves who arrange topics and the way of their interpretation according to their own views, values and policy adopted in the newsroom.

The issue of social influence may be defined as actions through which perception of reality is shaped in entities under its impact. According to Ratajczak, social influence is the process of making changes by an individual (or group) in another individual (or group) in order to achieve a certain goal. But social influence may also be perceived in terms of the effect on the recipient – adopting views or attitudes or enhancing them. What decides about the effectiveness of social influence are the recipient's competences and situational context [Ratajczak 2000: 5]. Situational context may have a different nature. Anna Kozłowska defines social context as a set of differentiated conditions in which communication takes place. At the same time, she points to a different possible nature of situational context. And thus she enumerates

1. social (media) context, which is connected with a certain reaction to the medium used in communication and its genre,
2. psychological context, which conveys the way the participants of the process perceive each other,
3. physical context, which describes the environment where the process of communication takes place,
4. cultural context, which is expressed by the adopted values and accepted behaviour in a given community,
5. historical context, which refers to historical past (negative or positive) of participants, which may influence the effectiveness of the communication process [Kozłowska 2006: 27].

Social influence of mass media has been studied since the 1930s. Initial research found a limited impact of the media on human attitudes and behaviour. It is a person's personality that constitutes a filter modifying the impact of messages from mass media to attitudes and behaviour of the individual. The way of processing information that come from the media is the effect of learning. Thus, the reception of content is different depending on what competences the individual has at their disposal. Social influences can have a varied nature – intended and unintended, explicit or implicit – and they may influence attitudes of recipients in a short or long term.

In the 1960s, there appeared a thesis developed by Joseph T. Klapper about the lack of influence of the media on recipients. Its author thought that mass communication is not treated as a necessary or essential condition to influence people. However, Klapper claimed that mass media mainly influence the existing views, enhancing them [Kunczik, Zipfel 2000: 151]. Factors generated by mass media and through which certain attitudes are enhanced include, according to Klapper, recipients' dispositions that decide about selective gathering and reception of information; social norms through which information is interpreted; the ability to influence public opinion; the structure of mass media in market economy, through which the same content is met with different reception – they create new ideas, enhance, weaken or modify the existing views of the recipients, or are completely neutral and have no influence on attitudes and views. Also Stuart Hall's encoding/decoding theory is based on negation of the recipients as passive viewers of TV programmes who uncritically and passively absorb the proposed content. In his theory, he introduced a four-step encoding and decoding model, consisting of production, circulation, distribution and consumption/reproduction. The content of the message is modified due to its circulation, in terms of both meanings and values. Media message in its content uses linguistic rules requiring proper communicational and cognitive competences of the recipient in the process of decoding the content itself. The broadcaster's aim is for the recipient to decode the content according to the dominating pattern. An element of the message is thus not only the existence of objective facts but also providing the direction for their evaluation through certain influence on the emotional side, which builds attitudes and behaviour [Hall 1987]. Andrzej Bełkot, analysing Hall's encoding/decoding model, points to two constituent elements of the communication act: "institutionalised broadcasting structure", which is responsible for encoding and distributing messages, and decoding, which triggers the structure of social practices. As he emphasises, the construction of the message is influenced, e.g. by the type of the used medium, or techniques used for constructing the message [Bełkot 2016]. Stuart Hall admitted that the picture of the world that is constructed by the media is ideological in nature and is subjected to the implementation of political goals in an economic, social or cultural context. Media messages suggest or even force preferred meanings and values. On the other hand, the news value theory is identified with the concept of news factor, which is the means of constructing the reality. News factors are features attributed to events and issues, making them media news, i.e. they become a construct worthy of informing public opinion about. Authors of the news value theory and at the same time first news factors were Johan Galtung and Mari Holmboe Ruge already in 1965, and later other factors were constructed. An issue will get news coverage if it has a certain value and simultaneously certain features stronger than other events – a higher level of negative emotions, an element of surprise or proximity of the problem, whose value is added by the media. In the news value theory there are three hypotheses: accumulation hypothesis – the more news factors the more probable it is that information will become the content of news coverage; complementarity hypothesis – the fact that one feature of an event is weaker, does not mean that it cannot be compensated with a strong participation of other feature; exclusion hypothesis – lack of news factors makes information worthless from the media point of view. Practical application of mechanisms described in news value theory makes the recipients get a distorted image of the world and reality they function in – the world is associated mainly with natural disasters or wars, and one's own backyard with fighting of the political elites and excessive exposure of celebrity activities. This adds to the cognitive dissonance also cultural distance, which is triggered by simplified and limited understanding of the other (without cultural contact), and it uses the known cultural divisions enhancing schemas and stereotypical thinking in recipients of media messages. Another theory that is also based on factors prompting selection of facts that become media news is framing theory. It means not only the choice of issues that makes the news but also their presentation in such a way as to highlight some facts and omit others, thus influencing public opinion. Robert Entman, Bertram Scheufele, Urs Dahinden and Jörg Matthes, who scientifically developed the framing theory, emphasised that this theory entails not only manipulating with content but also such a way of presenting the problem that the complexity of events and issues is reduced – one of the aspects is properly emphasised, others are ignored [Michalczyk 2013].

Another thesis is the conception of usefulness of the media proposed by Dennis McQuail, which assumes a few ways of using the media by recipients. And thus the utility of mass media means not only extracting information, building and enhancing the sense of identity of the individual, integrating and starting interactions in order to fulfil social roles and relaxing entertainment but also filling the leisure time [Mrozowski 1991: 245]. The typology proposed by McQuail, according to Anna Kozłowska, significantly defines the role of mass media in building social identity of a person, both in the personal and in the social dimension [Kozłowska 2006: 59]. Mass media are an instrument through which the recipients obtain fulfilment of certain needs and gain certain benefits from them. Media are forced to fight for the attention of recipients who give messages such values and meanings that reflect their needs. Anna Kozłowska emphasises that the content of information reflects the culture of the society where the message has been formulated, which means that the content of the media refers to the dominating message in a given society. Taking into consideration the growing diversity (including the one referring to multiculturalism) in societies, it is more and more often emphasised that media message is an interpretation of the reality and not its reflection. Also the recipients interpret and select the received messages in accordance with one's own views and needs. Social contexts are equally important, i.e. where the message is located or where the recipient reads it. Social contexts result from current political situation, social and economic phenomena and historical memory dominating cultural values for recipients. Processing of information received by the recipient takes place taking into account the foregoing context, one's own experiences (if the recipient has them), intellectual competences and the strength of emotions evoked by the analysed message. An important role that mass media play in the process of shaping identity, including cultural identity, also involves a certain force of drawing the recipients, usually through an attractive form of message, adjusted to the needs and expectations. According to Tal Samuel-Azran, the Al-Jazeera television, which is the soft-power tool in Katar's politics, is at the same time a way of reaching with a properly culturally built message to a Muslim community on a global scale [Azran 2016: 49]. It also serves as a spokesperson for the Muslim community in the international arena acting against propagation of the policy of bias and civilisation clash and presenting confrontational views rooted in religious differences. As he writes, for the residents of Western Europe, Al Jazeera is a reliable source of information about what is going on in the Middle East, simultaneously enhancing the identity of European Muslims. For the residents of the Middle East, this channel is a more important source of information than local national media [Azran 2016: 72]. In his typology of propagandist media, Robert Rajczyk includes such TV channels as Al Jazeera, the RT (formerly Russia Today), CCTV (China Central Television) into the so-called *narrative propagandist media*, i.e. the ones that broadcast external propaganda understood as a tool of digital diplomacy. As Rajczyk writes, propagandist media are aimed at presenting the point of view of their administrator, although they formally position themselves as objective journalism. Their propagandistic nature is the resultant of the used language and providing information in a carefully selected propagandist context [Rajczyk 2016: 75].

A particular form of communication that is used by mass media in order to shape attitudes and behaviour of recipients is persuasion. Persuasive communication, as a conscious and intentional action, influences the degree to which the recipients are informed, additionally forming their attitudes depending on the promoted patterns and shaping social needs. With persuasive communication through mass media, we can both enhance the existing attitudes and promote their possible modification. Another way of influencing recipients is manipulation, often consisting in misinformation, i.e. omitting information important for the recipient, often of statistical nature. The core of manipulative influence is the fact that the recipient is unaware that information which reaches them is incomplete (some of the information important for the presented situation has been omitted, withheld) or the provided facts are incompatible with reality. The recipient who does not have enough competences in the context of reading information has also limited possibilities of verifying their genuineness.

According to Jerzy Mikułowski Pomorski mass media have the ability to negotiate cultural content. Media are a tool for passing on information, an economic institution transmitting the public information they expect and a tool of implementing state or national policy. Mass media are a meeting place. As Mikułowski Pomorski emphasises, media communicate with the public in a mediated way, which means that codes of sociofugal communication and media communication may harmonise and then they enhance each other or they may compete and then the messages aimed at building the community are weakened [Mikułowski Pomorski 2007b: 20]. Within media culture, there function factoids, which do not exist in real reality in such a dimension as they are presented. Their task is creating or enhancing news by media for the purposes of the used communication channels, what follows from the characteristics of a given medium. Media implement state policies in the realm of multiculturalism. Tackling problems in certain contexts, they promote hate speech, reinforce stereotypes and prejudice against others. Another issue is instrumentalisation of anxiety following from the choice of the transmitted content. According to Grzegorz Mazurczak, mass media are traditionally the main source of obtaining knowledge about other cultures and social or political phenomena that take place in the world. As the author simultaneously emphasises, this educational mission of the media does not seem to be sufficient, mainly due to presenting messages in a way that does not show the full or real picture of the world and the existing problems. Distorted messages or understatements sometimes cause, according to Mazurczak: "*Unnecessary confusion in recipients, who are used to simple and unambiguous information*" [Mazurczak 2009]. In this context, the phenomenon of media racism (news racism) studied by Teun van Dijk is getting stronger. It is manifested in the lack of presence of migrants in the media or presenting them as a problem, not as part of the society like us. Migrants are stereotyped, marginalised in discussion or completely omitted. According to van Dijk, coverage about migrants is dominated by tendentious choice of issues, like criminality and other pathologies or deviations, deliberate formulation of headlines or choice of photos and words used to formulate messages. As Teun van Dijk emphasises, migrants' pathologies are exaggerated and the same behaviour of people belonging to one's own group is diminished. All this has an impact on building a consciously negative picture of a social group, which further influences political situation of the group by marginalising, isolating and exacerbating problems [van Dijk 2000].

In general, it should thus be stated that mass media appeal to sets of schemas existing in the recipients' consciousness and through which individuals interpret the obtained information. The so-called interpretative frames enable recipients ponder their place in the world, reject different values and enhance their own identity by relating to certain situations or events. Interpretative frames to a great extent are the resultant of the processes of socialisation and acculturation that take place in connection with globalisation and migration. If interpretative frames are rigid and the individual has limited possibilities of education, there is the possibility that they first and foremost use their own culture as a tool for interpretation of information that they get about the world. The ethnocentric attitude is thus enhanced and mass media do not serve the educational function in intercultural communication.

## 3.4 New Media and Their Significance in Contemporary Communication

The term "new media" denotes certain communication channels using the Internet. Since 2004, this term has been used to describe tools with a high level of interactivity. Tim O'Reilly called the changing behaviour of users the Web 2.0 era (collective intelligence). This means that Web 2.0 is a philosophy of designing and building Internet solutions aimed at using collective intelligence. On the other hand, Martin Lister emphasises that new media include methods and social practices of communication that developed thanks to digital and multimedia technologies, emphasising their features such as digitalisation, interactivity, hypertextuality, dispersion and virtuality [Lister, Dovey, Giddings, Grant, Kelly 2004]. According to Dominik Kaznowski, Web 2.0 is based on five basic assumptions:

1. The Internet is a platform joining people.
2. The Internet is a set of components (open standards).
3. Applications are not tied to specific devices or operational systems.
4. Applications are developed in an evolutionary way.
5. Open, light technologies are used for creating applications [Kaznowski 2010].

It is the users who become creators of content through being active on the Internet. The Internet has a social nature – content is created by users themselves, who publish their own opinions and views, share resources, build and keep up relations, are focused on informing, discussing and sharing content [Kaznowski 2010]. In communication, Web 2.0 users strive for dialogue, whose aim should be understanding, mutual respect, credibility and trust. Generally speaking, we may thus state that the aim of communication activities on the Internet is interaction. Such view is clearly supported by Manuel Castells' writing that new media make "*mass self-communication*" possible, which means horizontal, interactive communication networks based on the Internet, mobile phones, digital media and social websites [Castells 2007]. Media serve two principal aims: information (including gaining knowledge) and entertainment.

New media are also defined as an alternative for "old media" or "traditional media", as mass media are called. The essence of traditional media is mass transmission of information, reporting it and interpreting for recipients. On the other hand, new media have a social nature, users are not only observers of reality, but they can create information and also take part in its dissemination. According to Lyn Gorman and David McLean, the potential of new media lies in the radical transformation of relations between the media and their recipients, i.e. the consumers of content [Gorman, McLean 2009: 265]. But at the same time the authors claim that no social reconfigurations occur thanks to new media but what takes place there is merely a continuation of structures and processes from real reality. Thus communication in new media does not exert an important influence on social change, but it only replicates attitudes and actions occurring in real reality.

Mass media, i.e. "traditional media" are the subject of control in two areas – content and reception. Control is mainly institutional: traditional media channels have their owners who control both the message and their reception. Manuel Castells points to the significance of network control that takes place on the Internet. Also multimedia communication networks exert power and control over users. The difference lies in getting rid of control over dissemination of messages. These may be popularised beyond anybody's censorship. The conceptual framework presented by Castells indicates that monitoring on the network results in enabling or blocking access to messages. Similarly, as in the case of traditional media, power is concentrated on delineating the hierarchy of topics and taking decisions (allowing or blocking) by corporations managing communication networks. Thus, as Castells notes: "*Network-making power is the capacity to set up and program a network. /…/ The overarching goal of network management is to constitute the programmed*". Influence on programming networks, like in the case of traditional media, is exerted by owners and controllers of media corporations [Castells 2013: 412].

Dominik Kaznowski summarises the characteristics of social media in the following way:

1. They may be used at any scale.
2. Means of production are available for anyone interested.
3. Publication of information is only the beginning of the media process.
4. Original information may be modified indefinitely.
5. Access to the creation and reception of content is free.
6. Without social co-participation the idea of social media cannot be implemented.
7. Final value of information is directly influenced by participation of this social group (community) that is really focused around the tackled issue.

8. Each interested person has at any time access to their own and other co-creators' content and has the possibility to refer not only to the original content but also the input of other authors.
9. There is no coordination between authors.
10. All elements that are the effect of the process of creation (co-creation) of content are not removed and are always available.
11. Content is propagated by social interaction (what directly translates to the scale of distribution of each information).
12. The delay between the creation of content and its publication is maximally limited (there is no delay).
13. Unconstrained way of developing content [Kaznowski 2010].

According to Magdalena Ratajczak, both Manuel Castells and Barry Wellman emphasise social bonds that are created in network societies. Castells indicates that network bonds are usually much weaker than the physical ones but there are many of them and they do not exist in isolation from other forms of socialisation. Also Michel Maffesoli, the author of the concept of "neo-tribes", writes about strong ties shaped on the Internet. Among other things, this concerns ethnic diasporas that have a strong sense of group identity (Maffesoli 2008: 362). Communication functions in social media, that are the most popular communication channels in new media, are also noticeable in the area of their impact on shaping cultural awareness, the sense of national identity and pride of belonging to a certain ethnic group. New media are becoming an attractive communication channel between ethnic communities because access to these channels and promoting content through them is easier as compared to traditional media. Leah A. Lievrouw believes that media culture in a digital era has become more personal, sceptical, ironic, unstable and idiosyncratic, based on collaboration and extremely differentiated [Lievrouw 2012: 265]. Olga Bailey, Bert Cammaerts and Nico Carpentier outlined four theoretical approaches to alternative media. The first is community service. In this approach the aim is asserting the value in order to consolidate the community. Media tackle the most important issues for a certain social group, enable communication processes to those who are marginalised or stigmatised. In this way they create an alternative for mainstream media – they build an alternative model of presentation, at the same time creating own self-presentation and influencing the enhancement of the pluralism of messages. The third approach emphasises the role of alternative media, as part of civil society, enabling different social groups, also alternative ones, to participate in the public debate. The last approach, called a "rhizome", points to the interactivity of the media, where different movements are engaged, what influences the increase of independence of messages [Bailey, Cammaerts, Carpentier 2012: 39]. On the other hand, Leah A. Lievrouw emphasises the significance of the new media as alternative channels, engaged in processes of communication in their mediatory role. Lievrouw believes that thanks to the existence of networks there appear alternative and engaged projects that are usually characterised by a small scale of activity and cooperation of their participants, although sometimes projects create multimillion impact. Creators aim at building alternative subcultural spaces that function outside the main stream of the society and culture. One of the important tasks that are set before new media as a source of alternative projects is remediation, aimed at providing new meanings and changing ways of expression. Remediation is a process based on culturally existing forms of interaction that are introduced through new media, shaping social relations and cultural ties. Remediation may be of different nature. Its simplest manifestation is joining channels and content (new media consist of content available in traditional media). In this case remediation means the change of format. However, remediation also entails actions and forms of social and cultural engagement which encompass individual interactions, social relations, dissemination of content and using it. Remediation modifies and mediates, mixes content and ways of expression in order to create new relations, interactions and meanings [Lievrouw 2012: 269–271].

## 3.5 Characteristics of Communication in Social Media

Social research points to different effects of using the Internet, usually it is the weakening of relations in the real world due to more time spent in virtual reality. However, all the more often it is also proven that virtual contacts are complementary to relations existing in the real world. In the network there forms a supplement of social capital – contacts existing in real life are continued (with family, friends, acquaintances or people who are temporarily away physically, what is a barrier in keeping up personal relations). New media also have properties increasing participative capital – McCaughley and Awers' research of 2003 revealed that people active on the Internet are at the same time more engaged in social and participative issues [Skarżyńska 2009: 402]. A similar viewpoint is shared by Bart Cammaerts who emphasises the significance of social media during protests [Cammaerts 2015: 87]. Krystyna Skarżyńska, on the other hand, emphasises that the level of activity based on interaction is growing with the intensity (and seniority) of using new media – by participation in discussion groups, on-line chats and collective games [Skarżyńska 2009: 404]. Christian Garland emphasises the significance of protests as a form of participation, creating certain media events. He states that protests are a crystallisation of social antagonisms which become visible through the organisation of events, activation of individuals not only in the real world but also in the virtual one. Participation becomes the nature of the protest, also on the Internet [Garland 2015: 123][3]. Gemma Edwards draws readers' attention to political processes, which initiate cultural processes through social activation, creating new social movements [Edwards 2014: 77]. But Anna Kuczyńska notices that in the space of the Internet, there occurs conversation, from which there may arise opinion, extremely important for taking civic actions [Kuczyńska 2014: 13]. Opinion, what Gabriel Tarde has already noticed, stays in opposition to the crowd (as a social phenomenon, which is thoughtless in nature, spontaneous, easily gathered and equally easily dispersed). Gatherings are born from opinions, they make dissemination of opinions possible and they keep up their legitimacy. As Kuczyńska further notices, the network enables easy communication, what does not always make it possible for the opinion to form, but without a conversation the opinion is never formed. Numerous examples show that it is network communication, enabling opinions that are disseminated on the network to be created, that mobilises individuals to go out to the streets and articulate their social, political or economic expectations. Magdalena Dyła emphasises the share of blogs as tools of enhancing individualism and creating and participating in network discussion [Dyła 2011: 77–78]. The more so that both the number

3 Similar conclusions are formulated by G. Piechota and R. Rajczyk in the article The Role of Social Media during Protests on Maidan, *Communication Today*, 6(2).

of bloggers and significance of content they create are on the rise. It is often bloggers who are the first to reveal information that is later the subject of interest of traditional media. Also, more and more often, the representatives of traditional media resort to cooperation with bloggers in order to draw these Internet users who are not necessarily interested in content offered in traditional media. Cooperation with bloggers draws Internet users in front of TV sets [Gorman, McLean 2009: 280].

An important factor of social media influence on social structures is creating groups sharing the same views or values. Research of this issue was carried out by Michel Maffesoli, who coined the term tribalism created by social media connecting people in groups sharing the same values, views and ideas. Krystyna Skarżyńska, referring to Maffesoli's findings, writes that: "*using the Internet for social contacts makes it possible to check to what extent our opinions are shared by other users, to obtain new arguments to defend them, and it provides social validation of the correctness of our views and the sense of support: it turns out that there are people similar to us, who defend our beliefs. Internet users thus gain a sense of social acceptance and enhance their self-esteem and self-efficacy, what also brings about an increased share in real activities for the benefit of other people, public matters or institutions*" [Skarżyńska 2009: 404]. The Internet, as a tool and its channels as social websites, make public debate more shallow – instead of a dialogue there is quarrelling, and anonymity makes it possible to transform debates into conversations without any responsibility, often tinged with vulgarisms [Kotowicz 2006: 286]. A similar stance is taken by Manuel Castells who writes about the "*politics of show*" and emphasises flattening of the level of discussion and boils it down to spectacular net events [Castells 2009]. A well-known publicist Annie Appelbaum, in a text published at the end of 2015 in *The Washington Post*, accused the creator of Facebook – the most famous and widely used global social website – of destruction of the public debate and allowing the very notion of debate to devaluate, what directly negatively influences the development of democracy in the world, particularly in countries where it is relatively weak[4]. Similar accusations about devaluation of political discourse aided by the Internet

4 https://www.washingtonpost.com/opinions/mark-zuckerberg-could-spend-45-billion-on-undoing-facebooks-damage/2015/12/10/4b7d1ba0-9e91-11e5-a3

had been made earlier by Robert Samuelson in the same newspaper – *The Washington Post* – writing in 2006 that public debate has been made trivial, where the content of popular blogs run by amateurs is treated on a par with the views of political analysts [Keen 2007: 67]. However, talks on social channels also enable quick and instant access to information and make it possible for users to express their opinions, creating a democratic space for debate, particularly in the context of changes going on in the world, which increasingly condition the freedom of speech with the political changes influencing the mass media. Network communication does not like inequality and it does not eliminate dependence. The division existing in digital reality overlaps with social stratification and deepens it. This means that people who have a larger social, cultural or economic capital gain more on using the Internet than people with a lower level of these values. The exchange that occurs on the Internet is varied and it depends on competence levels. Economic deficit is the easiest to overcome – access to new equipment is not such a challenge as overcoming deficits in cultural or social capital. The deficit of values leads to a situation when users taking advantage of Internet possibilities limit their activity only to keeping up relations with others and to looking for entertainment [Bourdieu, Wacquant 2001: 79; Skarżyńska, Henne 2007: 172–186]. For such users, the Internet is not an important carrier of new informational and educational content.

## 3.6 Social Media in Intercultural Communication

The development of network communication makes it possible to create unlimited relations with other people, regardless of the place the individual is in. It is also theoretically possible to create relations with people belonging to different cultural circles. Pilot research carried out in 2014 revealed that such relations are not widely created using the network [Piechota 2014]. Only relations with people from other cultural circles existing in real reality tend to be transferred to virtual reality.

As Hofstede remarks, perceiving the superiority of technology over culture is an illusion [Hofstede 2007: 343–344]. Due to the development of

c5-c77f2cc5a43c_story.html?utm_term=.d31971653558 (accessed June 6, 2017). Applebaum 2015.

network communication, access to communication increases as well as the possibility of obtaining new data from different sources. But generally speaking, the skills of acquiring information are not changed, and according to Hofstede, there is also no change of cultural values. We read available messages in accordance with the preferred cultural values. As Hofstede notices, through the Internet we do things we would do anyway, but we do it quicker and more often. Moreover, the network does not influence the increase of tolerance and understanding, instead, differences are rather emphasised in communication processes. Michel Maffesoli had a similar view on the impact of the network on enhancing barriers between individuals and emphasising the differences when he referred to the impact of the Internet on social bonds. Technological progress only enhances tribal associations. Quoting Abraham Moles, the author of the term "*electronic galaxy*", he argues that the interactivity model where individuals connect creates tribal structures with considerably archaic features. The distinguishing feature of "*electronic galaxies*" is their temporariness. As Maffesoli emphasises, the essence of tribalism is enhancing what is near and being closed to otherness. But multiculturalism and multi-ethnicity characterising metropolises rather justify the phenomenon of uniformisation, also in the realm of culture, which to some extent rejects diversity. At the same time, in the realm of the so-called *urban mosaic* (the term coined by Ulf Hannerz), the multitude of micro-tribes created in the area of metropolises builds certain structures that tolerate or reject each other [Maffesoli 2008]. A similar view is shared by Jan van Dijk claiming that it is the same interests of members of the virtual community that create the community that is a heterogeneous collectivity, temporary in nature. Simultaneously, van Dijk states that the existence of virtual communities is often the effect of their functioning in an organic community. This means that networks have a limited ability to create unique communities and rather replicate those that exist in reality [van Dijk 2011: 234]. Jan van Dijk also emphasises that the network is not only a communication channel, but it also has the ability to create social environments where there are interactions and the combining of spheres and collectivities in a social context.

On the other hand, Manuel Castells in his theory of network society emphasises its global character and functioning in different cultural centres. Striving for the idea of community and individuality at the same time, according to Castells, has some consequences. Cultural identities become autonomous, what also makes them rejected by this part of the society that does not accept communitarianism of the network in the global dimension, preferring locality. However, in this context there occurs a problem connected with cultural diversity, which leads to fragmentation and which creates problems with communication of individuals with each other. Communication protocols between different cultures Castells mentions create security of the network. Without them, the network does not exist; there rather works a network structure, which stands in opposition to other communities. As he writes: "*the common culture of the global network society is a culture of protocols of communication enabling communication between different cultures on the basis not of shared values but of the sharing of the value of communication*" [Castells 2013: 49]. According to Castells, global culture is a culture of "*communication for the sake of communication*", which means that cultural networks interact, modify each other and not only coexist. Thus, through communication protocols, fear of the others is gradually overcome in the network exchange of intercultural nature. However, this process is relatively slow. Creating cosmopolitan culture currently concerns a small percentage of population (rather young people), and observation of current trends rather indicates reversed tendencies, i.e. the increase of nationalisms and using the "other" as a source of threat.

The issue of the Internet in intercultural communication is similarly perceived by Darin Barney, who acknowledges that in a network there occurs the fight for controlling cultural codes, through which it is possible to manipulate messages and manage discourses [Barney 2008: 154]. At the same time, Barney, like Castells, points that culture (its codes and symbols) is only the background or rather a tool for political fight to control individuals through the network. Quoting results of research carried out in the USA, Barney confirms, that the main purpose of network communication is keeping up relations with friends and family, looking for jobs and entertainment [Barney 2008: 152]. Denis McQuail, on the other hand, emphasises that in fact we still live in antagonistic nation states, under the influence of traditional mass communication, but new media influence the mixing of cultures and create new kinds of social networks [McQuail 2000: 481].

## 3.7 Tolerance in Network Communication

Aleksander Posern-Zieliński believes that intercultural dialogue through which common values are looked for and the space for cultural expression of each social group is created through negotiations leads to building multicultural societies, where despite the existing differences, tendencies for integration are stronger and they enable overcoming barriers and conflicts. An important element of intercultural dialogue is freedom of speech, allowing the right to criticise and negatively assess other cultures, behaviour or attitudes [Posern-Zieliński 2004: 41]. Political correctness that results from social pressure leading to balanced comments of individuals at the same time triggering self-censorship in individuals leads to a situation where many issues that are social problems are not solved but only seemingly resolved. The topic of intercultural communication, problems connected with diversity and prejudices resulting from contacts of people originating from different national, ethnic or religious groups, is an important problem in multicultural Europe, to which attention is drawn in different contexts. The Council of Europe, seeing the problem of prejudice that is rooted in different sources, in 2013 started the social campaign "No Hate Speech Movement"[5], aimed mainly at the elimination of hate speech on the Internet. Countries belonging to the European Union (EU), between which there is freedom of movement and residence, have different histories and experiences connected with multiculturalism. Still among the EU countries, there are such states where societies are ethnically homogeneous (or there is such an illusion) and where multiculturalism is a relatively new challenge. They include countries of the former Soviet Bloc, like Poland, Czech Republic, Slovakia, Hungary, where social attitudes shown to immigrants are completely different than those that are shown en masse by representatives of countries where societies have been multicultural for some time.

Multiculturalism is also starting to be perceived on more levels. From the traditional systemic understanding of multiculturalism as a structure created by people of different nationalities, cultures, ethnicity and religion who inhabit a given territory to perceiving family as a new scope of research in

5 Campaign's website: http://nohate.ext.coe.int/The-Campaign – accessed on 24.06.2014.

this respect. In families there are no borders of homogeneity of nationalities, cultures or religions of partners. According to Ulrich Beck and Elisabeth Beck-Gernsheim[6], in Germany about 20% of relationships are between partners of different nationality, ethnicity, religion or skin colour (in Berlin there are more such relationships). Often people with a different ethnic or cultural identity live in another country, which is not the country of origin of either of the partners. At the same time, multiculturalism is also the space for identification of new risks, sources of conflicts and looking for ways to tackle them. Risks resulting from the present can also be an element integrating people, regardless of their nationality or shared values [Beck 2002]. The risk society is being redefined in the face of constant individualisation, which means that only the individual becomes the subject of rights and obligations. This means that: "*opportunities, threats, ambivalences of the biography, which it was previously possible to overcome in a family group, in the village community or by recourse to a social class or group, must increasingly be perceived, interpreted and handled by individuals themselves*" [Beck, Giddens, Lash 2009: 20]. An individual is thus becoming more and more dependent on controlling their own possibilities, also the risky ones.

Social media play a very important role in creating new forms of multicultural relations. In a globalised world, they enable people to start relations with others in many different ways. Olga Guedes Bailey, Bart Cammaerts and Nico Carpentier define social media as alternative media that are concentrated on the concept of media serving the community – as such they are part of the civil society. In the context of understanding the community, not only in its spatial aspect but also the cultural one, alternative media serve the purpose of building a community of meanings, interpenetrations and images. As they claim: "*A community is actively constructed by its members and those members derive an identity from this construction*" [Bailey, Cammaerts, Carpentier 2012: 12]. Ulrich Beck and Elisabeth Beck-Gernsheim notice and describe the phenomenon of using the Internet to romantically connect people from different countries and cultures, thus influencing the creation of multicultural relationships. These relationships also come into existence as a result of taking conscious actions – looking

6 U. Beck, E. Beck-Gernsheim, *Miłość na odległość. Modele życia w epoce globalnej* [*Distant Love*], Wydawnictwo Naukowe PWN, Warszawa, 2013.

for partners representing a different national identity and cultural values. The problem of such relations is also a challenge for societies that have for many years been regarded as multicultural. The network becomes a tool of joining people in relations, regardless of the place of residence and one's own cultural identity. By emphasising the importance of project identities[7], Manuel Castells points out that their aim is changing cultural codes that create frameworks for communication in the network society. The result is changing the culture of virtual reality and supplementing it with alternative values [Castells 2009: 385]. David Dombrowsky notices the significance of social media in identifying the identity of an individual. He remarks that the identity in the individualised world is enhanced by social media, in the context of interactions, into which individuals get in communication activities. Confronting with users having other views or expressing different opinions or values, the individual enhances or modifies their own identity [Dombrowsky 2012: 91–103].

It seems, however, that the above theses about enhancing the identity of an individual, in confrontation with Maffesoli's idea of tribalism, build a kind of a training ground on the Internet, where representatives of polarised groups meet, fighting each other. According to Magdalena Ratajczak, who refers to surveys made by the Stefan Batory foundation, monitoring of the content published by Internet users in Poland shows a significant level of aggression towards ethnic, sexual and religious minorities. Results of other types of monitoring, periodically presented since 2011 by the Local Knowledge Foundation (Fundacja Wiedza Lokalna) in collaboration with the Collegium Civitas New Media Research Centre, show manifestations of racism, homophobia and xenophobia, most often aimed at Jews, Russians and homosexuals. The largest number of such activities has been reported on the gazeta.pl portal (Gazeta Wyborcza daily newspaper's portal). Since 2012, manifestations of hate speech have been noted also towards Muslims and Germans. But the most negatively marked statements invariably concern Muslims and Jews. Ratajczak also quotes the analysis of Internet forums in terms of hate speech. In this medium, negative opinions, offensive language

7 The importance of project identities as exemplification of political self-awareness and representation of different ideologies is also mentioned by D. Barney in *The Network Society*, Wydawnictwo Sic, Warszawa, 2008, pp. 172.

and cursing and racist statements are usually addressed to the Romanis, their customs and cultural distinctiveness. As Magdalena Ratajczak emphasises, anonymity allows such opinions, presenting virtual social attitudes of users. At the same time she writes that: "*Ethnic or religious groups rightly more and more often perceive the Internet as an alternative tool of communication. This is connected with a more difficult access to public and commercial media but also with an image of these groups in mainstream media. Such a form of communication creates new possibilities of shaping new transnational communities, international communication, building network identities. The Internet, as proved by numerous research, also enhances the existing identities, shaping new relations inside/within a group*" [Ratajczak 2014].

In the context of the above considerations, it is possible to assume that network communication and establishing international and intercultural contacts will in the future create new identity projects in real reality. All the more so, as Jan van Dijk remarks: "*the Internet does not replace existing communication modes but supplements them. /.../ the support given by networks and the rise of all kinds of weak ties along with the traditional strong ties create new communication groups, and even new types of communities*" [van Dijk 2010: 237]. But taking into consideration transferring relations existing in real reality to the Internet, including prejudice and stereotypes, we may expect that the creation of new identity projects (creating new communication protocols) will be hampered by obstacles connected with tribal association of users, exteriorised in virtual reality.

# 4 Empirical Aspects of Network Communication Processes in the Light of Migration and Cultural Differences

## 4.1 Research Methodology

Research that has been carried out for the purposes of this monograph was contextual in nature and it was carried out as the analysis of social reality in the context of self-reflection of respondents expressing their attitude to cultural contact with representatives of other national, ethnic or religious groups, to migration processes and one's own cultural identity in communication processes in new media. The communication processes were analysed from the perspective of the respondent's activity and entering into interactions with other network users. Declarations of the respondents that they formulated when they filled in the survey questionnaires were based on their opinions and were embedded in a subjectively perceived cultural context. Respondents' attitudes were analysed from a subjective-individual perspective (with the assumption that these activities are purposeful and they are rooted in the shared values), and an objective-social perspective (actions as a manifestation of practice shaped by discourses, traditions, adopted cultural and historical meanings).

Communication activities shaping public discourse may also be implemented through different channels, including the Internet. According to Seephen Kemmis and Robin McTaggart, communication activities are oriented at intersubjective agreement, mutual understanding and unstrained consensus. They create communication networks aimed at communication activities, whose task is to obtain the change of social practices, ways of understanding the situation and circumstances of actions [Kemmis, McTaggart 2010: 811]. Moreover, authors claim that practices in communication networks are connected with social movements grouping people as a response to unsolved social problems. These movements may be formal (problems expressed by non-governmental organisations) or informal (constituting a part of social order).

Malcolm McLuhan assumed that the medium is the message and this fact is extremely important for shaping or modifying people's perceptions of reality in which they function. Thanks to the media and the development of technologies the view of the world changes; there occurs a change of the system of communication, what in consequence leads to social changes. On the other hand, Manuel Castells confirms that the world is divided into the realm of the network and the self. The network is independent, lives its own life but most individuals concentrate their lives in the realm of the self, which is connected with places, where their life is really concentrated. This means that the identities distinguished by Castells (resistance, project or legitimation) are built in specifically located places and connected with certain situations concerning the individual.

During research attention has been paid to the auto-reflexive side of the respondents, who were asked for their opinions and attitudes, but the focus was also on the necessity to choose proper content the respondents agree with or reject. The aim of critical self-reflection was to make attitudes declared by respondents more strictly defined, also as a result of analysis of potential possibilities to choose from. Communication activities occur in specified social reality, what makes individuals often give in to social pressure or to imitate others. In this context, drawing the attention to different possibilities and emphasising the right to choose from the offered views was to let the individuals to indicate at this proposal that they really share or identify with.

The research topic is justified and it is the effect of rapid changes triggered by mass migrations of people, mainly from North Africa and Middle East to Europe, which have intensified since the second part of 2014. This phenomenon triggers different attitudes and activates different circles to take biased stances to migrants. A specific group are young citizens of European countries communicating with their surroundings through social media. Attitudes of these young people (in this monograph this means students), who live in large urbanised social structures, widely use new media and have the freedom of movement, are interesting from the scientific point of view, and strictly speaking from the angle of the analysis of changes that take place in their cultural identities as a result of communication processes in social media triggered with cultural contacts or only a "threat" of such contact.

Research for this monograph was carried out in the period of 2014 to 2016 in three stages. The following stages were not replications of previous ones, as each one had a different methodology, which was also prepared on the basis of the findings of previous research.

The first stage, which was a pilot study, was carried out in May and June 2014 in Berlin and Krakow. This research was made with the financial support of the Andrzej Frycz Modrzewski Krakow University. Trip to Berlin was financed as a study visit to the collaborating Protestant University of Applied Sciences in Berlin.

The pilot study was carried out on a group of two hundred randomly selected students, one hundred from each university. Students who participated in the study in Berlin came mainly from Germany. Besides German nationality, a few people declared other nationalities: Austrian, Italian, Turkish, Japanese, Spanish, English and Australian. The age of the students who took part in the survey was between 19 and 53 years and the average age was 28 years. The survey carried out in Krakow also included a group of students from Ukraine studying in the Andrzej Frycz Modrzewski Krakow University and residing in Poland. Students who took part in the survey in Krakow could be divided into two groups – over half of them were Polish and slightly over 20% were Ukrainians studying with them. One person declared Slovak nationality. Fourteen people did not declare any nationality. The age of the students who participated in the survey in Krakow was between 17 and 49, with the average of 22 years. Research was carried out with a quantitative method with the use of a survey questionnaire containing 34 questions, mostly closed-ended questions. The content of survey questionnaires was identical. Questionnaires used in Berlin were translated into the German language. The survey encompassed students of different years of study, in Berlin studying "social work" and in Krakow "journalism and social communication" and "management". The aim of the pilot study was to answer the following questions:

1. Do students notice multiculturalism in the environment they function in, and if so, how do they relate to the phenomenon of multiculturalism?
2. What are the sources of their knowledge about multiculturalism and who or what shapes their attitudes?

3. Do they use social media in processes of communication in the area of multiculturalism and do they treat these media as a source of education?
4. Do they feel threatened by functioning in a multicultural world? And if so, what is the source of their anxiety?

The results of the pilot study were published in the article Piechota 2014.

The second stage of research was determined by the rapidly changing situation, i.e. the mass inflow of immigrants to Europe and also a gradual increase of the nationalist climate, with its most marked effect so far being the referendum, when Britons decided for their country to leave the European Union (EU), and at the same time, also to limit the possibility of inflow of immigrants to their country. In this context, a decision has been made to do the survey in the same places where the pilot study was conducted, i.e. in Berlin and in Krakow. At this stage of research, two hundred students from each university, where in 2014 the pilot study was conducted, were invited to participate. Research was carried out with the use of a survey questionnaire containing 26 closed-ended questions in the period between April and June 2016. This research, similar to the one carried out two years earlier, was anonymous and it used the random sampling method. In both universities, students of social studies and humanities were asked about their attitudes. The survey questionnaire had the same content and it was translated into German for the purposes of the Berlin study. The participants of the German study comprised 65.5% women and 22.5% men, and in 24% of cases the respondents did not state their sex. Moreover, in Berlin, 84.5% of students were German and 3% of other origin (including Arabic, Turkish and Italian); in 12.5% of questionnaires, the origin was not stated. On the other hand, in Krakow, 68% of women and 28% of men took part in the survey, and in 4% of cases the sex was not stated. Like in the pilot study conducted in Krakow, a group of students from Ukraine studying in the Andrzej Frycz Modrzewski Krakow Academy and residing in Poland were also asked for an opinion and thus the respondents comprised 75% of Polish origin and 21% of Ukrainian origin, and in 4% of questionnaires the nationality was not stated. The projects in 2014 and in 2016 were carried out in the same universities but in different groups of students.

At the second stage of the project, students were asked to answer the following research questions:

1. Which information channels – traditional media or new media – are the source of information about the inflow of immigrants to Europe?
2. Do they identify radicalisation of attitudes leading to stronger nationalisms, with the root cause in the inflow of immigrants from the Middle East and Africa to Europe?
3. What are, in their opinion, the potential sources of threat for Europe, which stem from the inflow of immigrants?
4. Does a potential activation of nationalist attitudes take place in actual activities taken by the respondents or people from their environment or does such activation mainly take place in the processes of network communication?
5. Are social media more willingly used by students sharing negative opinions about multiculturalism in order to integrate in the face of threats, or conversely to organise aid for immigrants?

The third stage of research was carried out from October to December 2016 among students of three universities – in Berlin, Kiev and Krakow.[1] Justification for preparing the methodology for the third stage of research was the analysis of results of two previous surveys. The differences found in attitudes and the use of social websites in the communication of students were the reason to start the analysis of attitudes of respondents with reference to cultural differences, determining the types of cultures. At the third stage of research, the survey was also carried out in Kiev (Borys Grinchenko Kyiv University), in a group of Ukrainian students. The objective was to show possible differences in the processes of network communication that occur as regards the represented culture among Ukrainian students in Kiev and the ones studying in Krakow (who are simultaneously immigrants staying in Poland). The model of typology of cultures elaborated by Geert Hofstede was used to choose the three cultures (i.e. German, Ukrainian and Polish).

1 The deciding factor in choosing these three universities to do the research was their similar profile of education – humanities and social sciences. The Andrzej Frycz Modrzewski Krakow University and the Borys Grinchenko Kyiv University are in a group of medium-sized universities (over 10 thousand students) and they have a similar number of students, while the Protestant University of Applied Sciences in Berlin is a small university, with the number of students not exceeding two thousand.

*Chart 1: Typology of cultures according to Geert Hofstede*

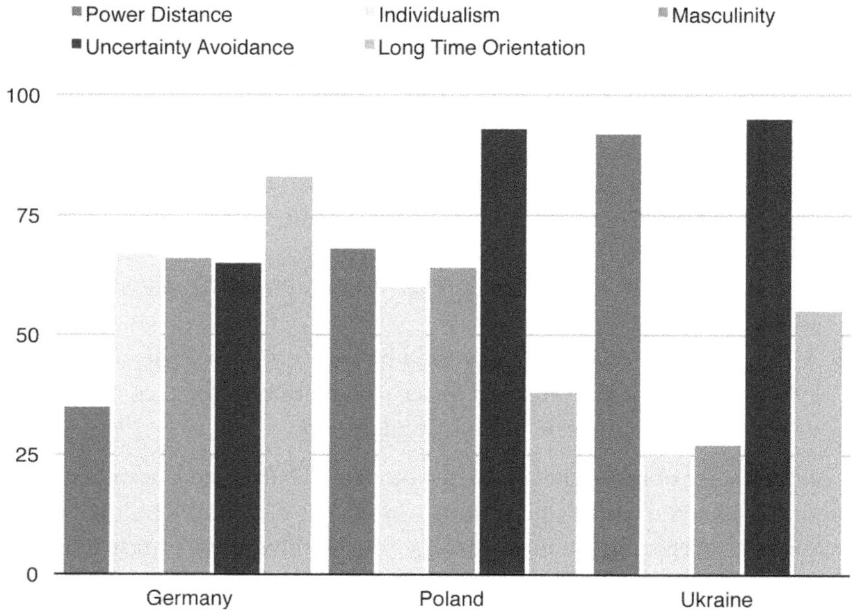


Own elaboration on the basis of Culture Compass – https://www.geert-hofstede.com/germany.html – accessed on 2.02.2017.

Chart 1 from Culture Compass locates cultures dominating in Germany, Ukraine and Poland as cultures differing in the defined criteria distinguished by Hofstede and which, at the same time, were taken into account when formulating the survey questionnaire for the third stage of research. While designing the third stage of research, it has been assumed that the typology of cultures prepared by Geert Hofstede will most effectively contribute to indicating cultural differences in network communication. As indicated by the author, the typology of criteria defining cultural differences (Chart 1) enables their transfer to research questions through which cultural differences are analysed in attitudes and communication behaviour of respondents. Moreover, the indicated typology identifies criteria based on cultural differences in communication processes, which are the subject of analysis also in this research. The representatives of three cultures took part in two previous research stages and the results showed significant discrepancies in attitudes and communication behaviour of students as regards intercultural communication, and also revealed own experiences of students from cultural contact with others, the attitude to immigrants and using social media in issues devoted to migration. The survey carried out in the third part of the project was aimed at revealing the role of social websites in the processes of cultural unification (if there are any) and their impact on promoting diversity originating in cultural differences. At this stage of research, the intention was also to answer the questions about whether it is possible to promote universal content (e.g. concerning human rights) through social websites or should messages be built in a different way for each culture to be effective. The research was an attempt to empirically prove the significance of social media in the processes of intercultural communication and their role in keeping up or changing the dominating cultural patterns that are the effect of the sense of cultural identity of the respondents. Social media are important in the processes of communication, as younger users use only these media, often not verifying and not confronting information found there with content propagated in mass media. Thus, it becomes important to answer the question to what extent the content propagated on the Internet is important for cultural unification and overcoming barriers concerning immigrants. Survey questionnaire that has been used at the third stage of research was built using the functional division of social websites. Its content, with 25 closed-ended questions and possibilities of choice for the respondent, was translated into German and Ukrainian languages and the survey was made among randomly selected students of different fields. Research questions for the third stage of the project were as follows:

1. Do students representing different types of cultures approach differently the choice of network communication channels and creating content?
2. How do the respondents react to the message with a certain content in low- and high-context cultures?
3. Can universal content be promoted through social media or is content of messages culturally conditioned?
4. Does using social websites influence the change of attitudes and communication behaviour of students representing different types of culture?

At the third stage of research, the sample comprised students distributed in the following proportions: in Berlin, 76.29% women and 23.71% men;

in Krakow, 81.63% women and 18.37% men; and in Kiev, 90% women and 10% men. Students participating in the study were of different ages. In Berlin, 70.98% of respondents were aged 18–25 and 29.02% were over 25. In Krakow, 84.67% of respondents were aged 19–25 and 15.33% were over 25. In Kiev, mainly very young students participated in the survey, 96% of which were aged 17–20 (Ukrainians start university education at 16 to 17 years of age). Students participating in the study resided in cities with a different population. 11.34% of students from Berlin came from smaller cities with up to 50 thousand residents, 22.45% of students from Krakow and 34% of students from Kiev. Residency in cities with a population of 50 to 100 thousand was declared, respectively, as follows: 7.22% of respondents in Berlin, 18.88% of respondents in Krakow and 12% of respondents in Kiev. In big cities with over 100 thousand residents, students from Berlin constituted 81.44%, from Krakow 58.67% and from Kiev 54%.

Research was carried out in three cities. These were selected due to their size and social and cultural differentiation, which are the features of large cities. Berlin as a multicultural city is currently inhabited by representatives of about 180 nationalities from all over the world. Krakow is the city with historically conditioned multiculturalism, which is currently more and more often resorted to make this place attractive for people from other parts of the world coming for tourist, educational or professional purposes [Soja, Zborowski 2011: 227]. Krakow is also an important place for migrants to settle. Krakow's ethnic structure currently comprises representatives of several nationalities, with the most numerous being Ukrainians. Others include, e.g., Belarusians, Slovaks, Czechs, Armenians and ethnic minorities Romanis and Lemkos [Soja, Zborowski 2011: 226].

Kiev is a multicultural city, what is mainly the effect of historical and political conditions. Russians, Poles and representatives of other post-Soviet republics live in Kiev.

## 4.2 The Role of New Media in Overcoming Stereotypes and Prejudices of Students

Pilot study carried out in 2014 in Berlin and in Krakow pointed to important differences in perceiving multiculturalism by students of each university.

Differences were also identified in using channels in social media for intercultural communication.[2]

Students in Berlin declared less frequent contacts at their university with representatives of other national and ethnic groups than their counterparts in Krakow.[3] At the same time, the respondents in Berlin more often emphasised that they did not pay attention to where other students come from. Similarly, in declarations of the respondents concerning who they keep closer relations with, it was students from Berlin who more often pointed to people from other national or ethnic groups than the respondents in Krakow. Students in Berlin also less often answered that they pay attention to their friends from other national or ethnic groups around them, what may prove that functioning in a multicultural environment makes such relations so common that some respondents do not pay attention to the origin of their friends.

On the other hand, analysing whether students of both universities know people of other nationalities or ethnic groups, respondents both from Berlin and from Krakow indicated a similar level of personal relations (in Berlin 89% and in Krakow 88%). The difference was that among the respondents in Berlin a larger group declared not paying attention to origin. Declarations of students as regards spending time with people coming from different countries or ethnic groups looked quite different. People surveyed in Krakow much more often declared the lack of such relations. On the other hand, people in Berlin regarded spending time together as normal (91% of positive answers in Berlin and 57% in Krakow). Students were also asked if their knowledge of culture of other countries increased as a result of personal contacts with representatives of other cultures. Respondents in both cities indicated that their knowledge about culture increased (78% of positive answers in Berlin and 60% in Krakow). At the same time, analyses

2 Full study report is available in the article The Role of Social Media in Creating Intercultural Dialogue and Overcoming Prejudice – A Comparative Analysis of Pilot Survey Results, published in *KOME – An International Journal of Pure Communication Inquiry*, 2014 2 (2): 37–63, http://komejournal.com/files/Piechota%20KOME.pdf – accessed on 4.01.2017.

3 This difference is due to the fact that at the university in Krakow where the study was conducted, there studies a big group of students from Ukraine (in the survey, about 20% of respondents were Ukrainian).

proved a higher level of individualisation of relations of students from Berlin with people coming from other cultures, because these students more often answered that they were interested in contacts with people and not in their origin. The research also sought to find the relationship between the sense of security of the respondents and living in a country with people of other nationalities or ethnic groups. Students both in Berlin and in Krakow in general did not treat these people as a threat for themselves, but a higher level of insecurity was declared by students from Krakow. On the other hand, the respondents in Berlin more often emphasised that they were simply not interested in these issues. This may mean that they notice the threat, but they do not see its source in the origin of people. It is also interesting to look at the potential sources of feeling threatened. Respondents both in Berlin and in Krakow admitted that the source of insecurity results from the fact that another religion that will become dominant will impose a certain model of living on them. Their fears also stem from the fact that people coming from other cultures with a different system of values will decide about students' life. According to students from Berlin, the inflow of new workers who might take over workplaces is not perceived as a threat. Students from Krakow feel threatened with the inflow of workers from other countries who might take over their workplaces. These differences should rather be interpreted as a subjective assessment of the labour market by the respondents (students in Krakow were rather convinced that the inflow of cheap labour will not only impact the ability to find work but also lower wages). Students in each city were also asked if they had ever fallen victim to violence motivated by their nationality or ethnic origin. Students in Berlin more often said yes to this question (29% answers) than students in Krakow (12% answers). These answers are particularly interesting in juxtaposition with data concerning the sense of security of students in each city. Students in Krakow declared more fears connected with the sense of security although, at the same time, they less often fell victim to violence connected with nationality, skin colour, practiced religion or declared views. Analysing the nature of violence the students have fallen victim to, in the case of people from Berlin, it mostly included public comments and insults, exclusion from the group the student had participated in and beating (single answers). Quite rarely students said about hate speech towards them on the Internet. On the other hand, students in Krakow answered that it was aggression and hate speech on the Internet that were the basic source of violence against them. A few students also said that violence against them consisted in public insults and negative comments about them in real reality.

Students who fell victim to violence in Berlin were Germans aged 22–25, an Austrian man, people of Spanish and English origin, as well as a Japanese and a Turkish person (one answer). On the other hand, among students in Krakow, the victims of violence were Poles (aged 22–40) and Ukrainians (aged 19–22).

Students were also asked about manifestations of violence motivated by national or ethnic differences to people from their environment. A difference in experiences of people in each city could be noticed. In Berlin, 39% of respondents revealed that people from their environment fell victim to violence, whereas in Krakow, 19% of respondents revealed so. Students in both cities mostly fear people from the Muslim culture. Moreover, the respondents in Krakow emphasised that they also fear people from the Far East, from Central and Eastern Europe and the inhabitants of Sub-Saharan Africa.

Attitudes of students to sharing the same space with people from different cultures also seem interesting. Most students are ready to share a flat with a person from another nationality and ethnic group (54% of answers in Berlin and 64% in Krakow), while the respondents in Krakow more often gave negative answers (8%); they also less often declared that their decision depended on a particular person, i.e. individualised choice (this possibility was marked by 42% of respondents in Berlin and by only 28% in Krakow). This may be the evidence of the fact that the level of prejudice and being guided by stereotypes strongly influences attitudes of respondents in Krakow. During analysis, the answers of students were confronted; the questions sounding differently but concerning the same topic were put in different places of the survey questionnaire in order to make the pervious answers more probable. Verification confirmed attitudes of students from Berlin but revised attitudes of the respondents in Krakow, showing a higher level of prejudice to sharing a flat with people who are members of other national, ethnic or religious groups. Among answers with whom the respondents rule out living with, the respondents from Berlin suggested the followers of Islam. However, among the revealed preferences of students in Krakow, living together with people who practice Islam is ruled out, as well as the Romanis, Jews, Germans, Ukrainians and Africans (without stating who specifically these people had in mind). What is interesting, in the case of the group of respondents from Krakow the analysis was also made on the basis of answers obtained from Poles and Ukrainians. The first group of people with whom the possibility of sharing a flat was ruled out included the Romanis, Muslims, Jews, Germans, Ukrainians and Africans, whereas the other group included the Muslims, Catholics, Russians and Poles.

The above analysis proves that the main source of prejudice, as regards students both from Berlin and from Krakow, is first and foremost religious differences. Among Poles, research also revealed individual anti-Semitic attitudes (people who said that they rule out living with a person of Jewish nationality were aged between 35 and 45).

Another research problem was the analysis how travelling to countries outside the EU influences the respondents' experiences. Students from Berlin had more experience connected with travelling outside the EU than students from Krakow (86% of answers in Berlin and 72% in Krakow). Answers concerning the longest period of staying abroad in the case of students from Berlin include a period of up to two weeks; there are also answers pointing to a period of up to a month or three months. The most common reasons for travelling were holidays, then education or vocational apprenticeship, visiting friends or family or working abroad. On the other hand, among students from Krakow, the period of stay was not longer than two weeks, less often up to a month. The reasons of the stay were most often holidays or visiting family or friends. Juxtaposing answers to questions about travelling abroad with fears of people of other nationalities or ethnic groups, we obtained the result that travelling abroad (with the most often given reason being going on holidays) does not help overcome prejudice and fear. Students who expressed fear and prejudice against others mostly included these people who travelled on holidays and their fears mostly concerned Muslims (the largest number of answers); individual answers concerned the residents of Africa in general.

The last portion of the presented survey results concerns the influence of traditional media, also statements of politicians in the media, on shaping students' attitudes in each city. Answers concerning the activity of students in social media were excluded from the analysis, as they are a separate type of mass medium that may be a place for self-education of students. Students both in Krakow and in Berlin have similar attitudes towards messages concerning multicultural Europe presented in traditional media. Students both in Berlin and in Krakow rather answered that they did not watch/listen or did not remember programmes that would tackle the issue of a multicultural Europe. There were differences in students' opinions about statements of politicians in traditional media (radio, television). Students in Krakow stated that programmes they watch are highly political, contrary to the students from Berlin (research was carried out in the period May-June 2014 – author's remark).

The survey revealed slight differences in using social media by students from Berlin and Krakow. German students use social media less actively than their Polish and Ukrainian peers. This may be the result of different ages of students – average age of students from Berlin who participated in the study was 28 years and average age of students from Krakow was 22.

The most popular communication channels in social media were YouTube and Facebook among students from Berlin and Facebook, YouTube, Instagram and Twitter among students from Krakow. A vast majority of respondents declared that they have people of other nationalities or ethnic groups among Facebook friends (77% of respondents in Berlin and 76% in Krakow). However, more students from Krakow said no (18% answers), while in Berlin, students did not remember if they had such friends (19% answers). This would confirm earlier research findings that the respondents in Berlin pay less attention to nationality of their friends, also on the Internet. Usually people who know each other in person or have mutual friends, at the same time, become friends on Facebook. In the case of students from Krakow, the diversity of reasons for which the respondents get into contacts with others was wider. The analysis of activity on the Internet revealed differences in the interest in multiculturalism in respondents in both cities. In Berlin, respondents more often declared looking for and analysing content devoted to multiculturalism on the Internet, whereas students from Krakow actually revealed lack of interest in this topic. Also, students' attitudes expressed in belonging to groups and communities on Facebook are different. The respondents from Berlin were more often participants of groups and communities that were devoted to intercultural dialogue, promoting tolerance in a multicultural world and supporting integration of immigrants in new environment. However, the respondents in Krakow most often pointed to lack of interest in this issue. Additionally, it should be emphasised that students from both cities rather do not declare negative attitudes to the creation of multicultural states – the lowest index concerned participation in groups and communities that gather users around the idea of opposition to building multicultural states.

## 4.3 Summary of the First Stage of Research

To sum up, the carried out pilot study revealed differences in attitudes of students from Berlin and Krakow. Students in Krakow pay more attention to multiculturalism of the environment they function in. On the other hand, students from Berlin treat multicultural environment as natural, and individualisation of relations is also more noticeable among them. Interestingly, negative experiences, like being the victim of violence motivated by nationality, ethnicity, skin colour, views or religion, are to a greater extent shared by students in Berlin than in Krakow. At the same time, the former declare a much lower level of prejudice than the latter. This may provoke a conclusion that one's own experiences, even negative ones, do not lead to increased prejudice and fear, also due to individualisation of social relations. On the other hand, lack of own experiences triggers stereotypes and prejudice that replace even negative but real experiences.

Students in Krakow pointed to a much higher level of political content of messages in electronic media – on the radio and on TV. At the same time, in the case of both groups of students, it has not been established that politicians' statements influence the shaping of different attitudes; they can, however, have impact on preserving schemas and prejudices as well as reinforcing fears in these individuals who have no own experience or have it limited to cultural contact with representatives of other national or ethnic groups. In the case of both groups of students, the source of prejudices were fears connected with religious differences and potential influence of another religion that is based on a different axiological system on everyday life of an individual. Respondents in both cities emphasised that their fears and prejudices are mainly directed against people practising Islam.

Students in Krakow more often communicate with the use of social media than students in Berlin. The latter at the same time declared that they more often used social media to search for information connected with multiculturalism, promoting tolerance and helping immigrants to assimilate with the society. At the same time, both groups declared a rather low level of interest and activity in groups, whose aim is opposing to building multicultural societies. On the other hand, the analysis how students in both cities use communication channels in social media has shown that they do not use them to start new relations but only to move relations existing in real life to the Internet. At this stage of research, we thus cannot definitely say that activity of students in social media influences overcoming stereotypes and eliminating prejudice. However, the survey made it possible to formulate a conclusion that students from Berlin living in a multicultural environment are less prejudiced and less fearful of multiculturalism than students in Krakow (Poles and Ukrainians), for whom multiculturalism is still a social challenge. This proves that living in a multicultural environment, despite experiencing violence more often, helps individualisation of relations and perception of people of other nationalities, ethnic or cultural groups individually and not only through the prism of schemas. We may assume that students from Krakow (Poles and Ukrainians) who have less cultural contact with other values are more often driven by fears and stereotypes when defining their attitude towards the environment, which is the result of a cognitive deficit in this respect.[4]

To sum up this part of the study, it should be stated that declarations of students revealed in the survey confirmed that functioning in a multicultural environment influences the reduction in the cognitive deficit, which, if it exists, simultaneously influences the increase of anxiety and triggers stereotypes in the respondents.

---

4 According to Walter G. Stephan and Cookie W. Stephan: "When a stereotype is activated it can trigger the mechanism of a self-fulfilling prophecy. This process consists of three stages. First, people are prone to look for such information that will confirm their expectations. Second, information confirming the stereotype draws attention better and is better coded, unless the evidence contrary to the expectations is strong and unambiguous. Even if the information undermining the stereotype is remembered, it will probably not be attributed to internal factors and, moreover, the person who does not fit the stereotype is often disliked. Third, expectations resulting from a stereotype influence human behaviour, increasing the possibility that a representative of a foreign group will react in a way confirming the expectations" (p. 42). More in *Intergroup Relations*, Gdańskie Wydawnictwo Psychologiczne, Gdańsk, 2003.

## 4.4 The Significance of Social Media in Shaping Students' Attitudes to Immigrants

The main information channels students draw knowledge about migration from in both cities are television and Internet portals, which are presented in Chart 2.

*Chart 2: Sources of students' knowledge about migrations*

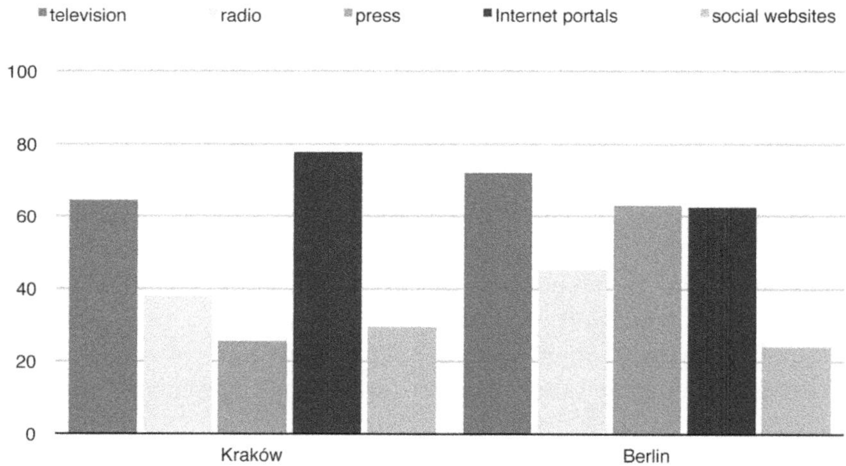


Own elaboration.

Students in Krakow much less often than students in Berlin turn to press as a source of information concerning the issue of immigrants, but slightly more often use Internet portals. Among social websites, the respondents most often indicated Facebook (24% in Berlin and 28.5% in Krakow). Other individually indicated sources of information were other social websites, like Twitter and YouTube, and direct communication, i.e. talking with family and friends or personal experiences of a student that he or she treated as a source of information about immigrants.

The respondents were asked if in connection with the mass inflow of immigrants to Europe they consider this phenomenon a threat. Answers to the same question asked to respondents in two cities were totally opposite. Over 80% of students from Krakow answered that the inflow of immigrants to Europe is a threat (12% had an opposite opinion and 7.5%

did not know). In the case of students from Berlin, the answers had an exactly opposite distribution. Only 11% of the respondents answered that the inflow of immigrants was a threat (81.1% thought opposite and 7% did not know). Pointing to potential dangers, the respondents both in Krakow and in Berlin thought that the increased terrorist threat was the main and basic problem. A larger group of students from Krakow indicated cultural dissimilarity that may influence their life and fear for the loss of workplaces that immigrants will take over. Detailed opinions of students about sources of threat are presented in Chart 3.

*Chart 3: Students' concerns connected with migration*

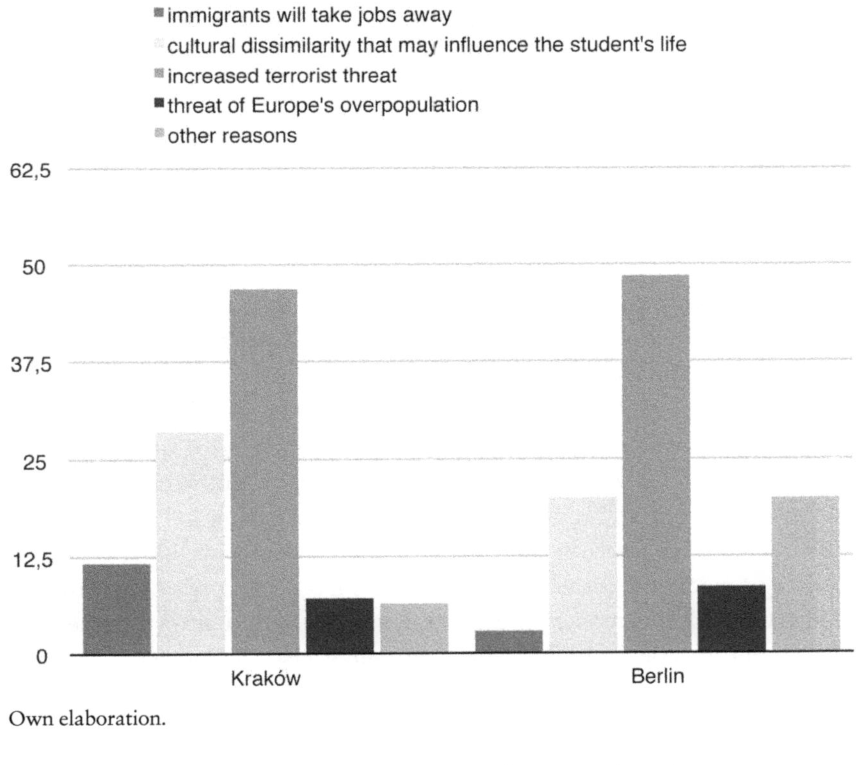


Own elaboration.

Analysing personal engagement and participation of students in protests that were organised against the inflow of immigrants to Europe, it seems that students both in Berlin and in Krakow did not reveal their engagement in such actions. Only 1% of respondents in Berlin and 1.5% of respondents in Krakow declared that they took part in protests in person. Students pointed, however, that they knew people who actively participated in such protests. Such an answer was given by 16% of the respondents in Krakow and by 54.5% in Berlin. First, this means that Berlin is a city where such protests take place more often than in Krakow and citizens are actively engaged in them. Second, it confirms findings of the earlier pilot study that students in Berlin function in a more diversified cultural environment, at the same time retaining and demonstrating their own individual attitudes.

Participation of the respondents in actions that were aimed at supporting the policy dedicated to helping immigrants was analysed in the study. Responses to this question also differed. Only 1% of students from Krakow declared such an activity, while in the case of students from Berlin active support for immigrants was given by 23.5% of respondents. This means that students from Krakow are not active in protests against immigrants and in helping them.

Analysing students' attitudes to immigrants and their significance for the future of Europe, the respondents in each city were asked for opinions about whether the inflow of immigrants may positively impact the development of European countries. Only 15% of students from Krakow and as many as 77% of their peers from Berlin said yes. This discrepancy may be mainly the effect of experiences of each country. In Berlin, the respondents may observe and evaluate if their city benefited by the inflow of immigrants (also counting earlier migrations to Berlin). In Poland, the issue of the share of foreigners in the labour market is still not an important subject of public debate. The group of immigrants from Ukraine working in Poland, which is estimated at about one million people and gradually growing, is not the subject of media coverage. It could enable shaping people's own attitudes connected with the impact of migration on the labour market and the level of the country's development. Another issue is also the impact of cultural diversity, which is manifested in different aspects of development and which is still not really noticed by Poles.

Answers of students showing their participation in the discussion that took place throughout last year and concerned the problem of migration were also quite interesting. Over 80% of respondents from Berlin answered that they took part in such a discussion, compared to students from Krakow, 52.5% of whom gave positive answers. The discussions were mostly personal exchanges of opinions. This answer was given by 73% of respondents from Berlin and 52.5% from Krakow. Chart 4 presents in detail how the answers in each group of students were distributed.

*Chart 4: Places of students' discussions about migration*

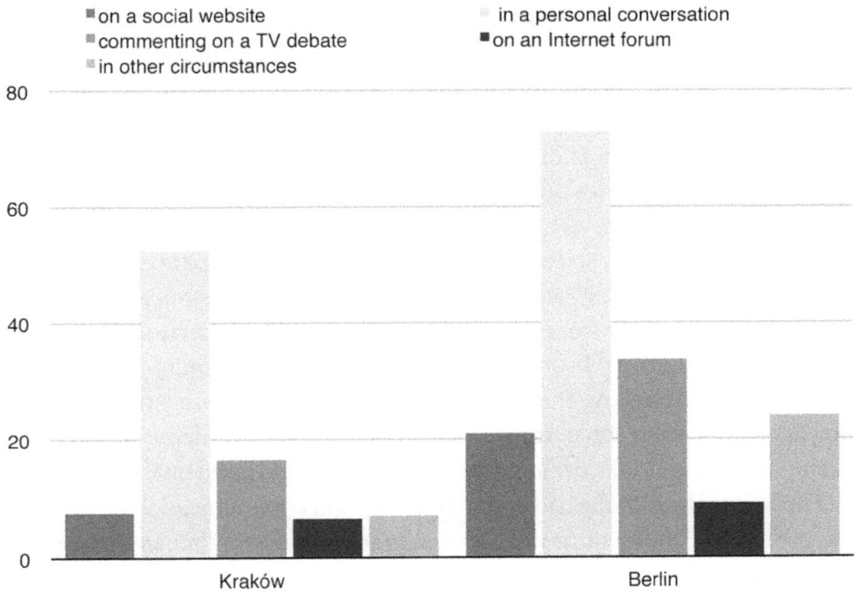


Own elaboration

The general conclusion that can be drawn from this analysis is that both in personal conversations and when using social websites to exchange opinions about migration, respondents from Berlin were more engaged. We may assume that this results not only from greater interest in this issue (Berlin is one of the cities with a big inflow of immigrants) but also that this issue is more often the subject of media analyses, e.g. debates on TV. In personal conversations, particularly those held among family, we may assume that cultural patterns shaping a certain attitude to immigrants are rather replicated.

On the other hand, as far as the discussion devoted to the issue of migration on social websites is concerned, the most popular channel remains

Facebook, where respondents usually exchange opinions on their friends' profiles (this also means that they do not create their own content about this issue and do not initiate discussions but only take part in them). Such activity was declared by 13% of respondents in Berlin and 6% in Krakow. Initiating discussions on one's own Facebook profile was declared by only 3.5% students from Berlin and 1.5% from Krakow. Also, as regards other places of holding discussions – the fan page of a non-governmental organisation (indicated by 8% of respondents from Berlin and 3.5% from Krakow), and the community on Facebook the respondent is a member of (7.5% in Berlin and 4% in Krakow) – the engagement of students in Berlin and in Krakow is different. Students in Berlin were more engaged in using social websites for discussions about multiculturalism and the problem of migration.

The subject of interest during the survey was the participation of students in a network happening, which was aimed at taking the stance supporting immigrants or, on the contrary, showing protest in connection with their mass inflow to Europe. From Berlin, 20% of respondents pointed to participation in the happening that took place on a social website (students were not asked to reveal what stance they took). Among students in Krakow, such participation was declared by only 3.5% of respondents.

Further analysis of the use of social websites in communication devoted to the problem of multiculturalism and migration revealed that students were asked if in the last year they became members of new groups or communities on Facebook, including those that are devoted to the theme of multiculturalism and mass inflow of immigrants to Europe. Membership in such new groups or virtual communities was declared by 23% of students in Berlin and by 10.5% in Krakow. At the same time, 43% of students in Berlin and 40% in Krakow declared becoming members of new groups and communities. This result shows that on average every one in two network activities of a student in Berlin and one in four of a student in Krakow concerned becoming a member of a new group or network community whose subject of concern is the issue of multiculturalism and migrations. In this context, students were asked questions specifying their network activity concerning participation in discussions devoted to the issue of multiculturalism. And thus the question if the respondent during the previous year joined a network community that is engaged in organising aid for immigrants was answered positively by 27.5% of students in Berlin and 5.5% in Krakow. And the question if students are engaged in sharing content on social websites (photos, films) that concern the issue of migration was positively answered by 19% of respondents from Berlin and 15.5% from Krakow. At the same time, students were not asked if they shared online content supporting immigrants or expressing protest against migration.

The sources of information about immigrants for students are also blogs, the use of which was declared in Berlin by 18.5% of respondents and in Krakow by 32.5%. In this group of users, i.e. readers of blogs, in Berlin 46.9% and in Krakow 21.5% of students analyse blogs where the problem of migration is tackled. Among the readers of blogs about migrations, 88% of respondents in Berlin and 71% in Krakow pointed that the blogger is revealing their personal attitude to the issue which the respondents agree 100% with. This attitude expressed by respondents confirms the theory of tribalism on the Internet formulated by Maffesoli, in which individuals are more often prone to participate in these groups where their opinions are agreed with. Respondents were also asked about their attitudes concerning the policy of accepting migrants. More than 68% of students from Berlin opposed the toughening of the policy of accepting immigrants, whereas 75.5% of respondents from Krakow pointed to the need of increasing safety of citizens and toughening immigration policy. This result shows a quite paradoxical situation in which students in Berlin, where part of the wave of migration has been channelled since 2014, do not see the need to toughen immigration policy, whereas students in Krakow, where the problem practically does not exist, think it is necessary. It seems that the most probable conclusion that may be made as the interpretation of the result is fear of the respondents in Krakow for mass migrations that reach Europe. This conclusion would also confirm earlier findings from the pilot study, which revealed that one of the main fears that students from Krakow have is the impact of cultural otherness that the immigrants bring directly to their life. It is different in Berlin, where for many years it has been possible to meet in the streets thousands of people from different cultures, national and ethnic groups, with whom public space is shared.[5] Lack of experience of the

5 In Berlin, there currently live the representatives of over 180 nationalities.

respondents from Krakow seems to be the main source of fear, particularly in connection with the educational deficit and media messages in the Polish television, which are usually concentrated around presenting negative information connected with migrants and their presence in the European public space.

As an attempt to define the attitude of students in each city to immigrants, a few sentences have been formulated and the students were asked to mark the ones they agree with.

Juxtaposing the results, we may draw the following conclusions:

1. 90.5% of students from Berlin and 21% from Krakow think that immigrants should be helped, which stems from the humanitarianism principle.
2. 9% of students from Berlin and 60.6% from Krakow think that immigrants should reform their own countries and not run away from them.
3. 33% of students from Berlin and 38% from Krakow think that the main reason for migration is the will to live a more comfortable life.
4. 28% of students from Berlin and 20.5% from Krakow think that politicians and media in their statements terrorise societies, using the problem of migration for this purpose.
5. 0.5% of students from Berlin and 22.5% from Krakow believe that the inflow of immigrants will destroy European civilisation.
6. 0.5% of students from Berlin and 10.5% from Krakow think that monocultural countries, where the problem of social stratification does not exist, develop better.
7. 76.5% of students from Berlin and 21.5% from Krakow think that immigrants may positively influence the development of European countries, including their own.
8. 65.5% of students from Berlin and 49% from Krakow think that the problem of immigration should be treated individually and each immigrant should be regarded as an individual being.

Attitudes revealed by the respondents show that students in Berlin, similar to the earlier pilot study, have richer experience resulting from living in a diversified environment, which leads to greater empathy and understanding of the situation of immigrants, the attitude to which is more individualised. Another issue is the perception of the role of immigrants as the driver of economy, what significantly influenced the development of Germany already in the 1970s. Anxiety mentioned earlier as a social emotion felt by students in Krakow also generates lack of empathy. The idea that the immigrants should themselves care for their fate results both from the refusal of a large group of students to provide aid stemming from the idea of humanitarianism and from acknowledging that immigrants should reform their own countries and not look for a comfortable life outside them. What's interesting, students in Berlin also assumed that some immigrants want to live more comfortably and this is the reason of their migration, but there were no emotions connected with it, as a result of which they would refuse to help immigrants.

Respondents were also asked what mechanism of influencing others that may be used in the processes of communicating about immigrants they find the most effective (the channel was not stated). Out of a few sentences pointing to different mechanisms of social influence and creating attitudes in public opinion that were proposed to the respondents, students in Berlin chose the presentation of political and social situation in countries the migrants come from (64% of answers in Berlin and 35% in Krakow) as the most effective mechanism. The second most effective mechanism of influence chosen by students in Berlin was appealing to the general principle of humanitarianism, which makes people help others (26.5% of answers in Berlin and 20.5% in Krakow). Another answer was using visual messages (pictures and photos) as a form of influencing attitudes and it was students from Krakow that treated them as more effective than students in Berlin (15.5% of answers in Krakow and 6.5% in Berlin). The last of the proposed sentences concerned imitating celebrities in order to influence the shaping of attitudes of other people was treated as effective by more respondents from Berlin (10.5% of answers in Berlin and 9.5% in Krakow).

Analysing answers given by students in both cities, we may state that they confirmed previous research findings. In answering the questions, respondents in Berlin were more often driven by empathy and they pointed to the necessity of learning and understanding the situation the immigrants found themselves in. But much less often than in Krakow, students in Berlin revealed being manipulated by content in the form of specially selected pictures (presenting touching scenes with women and children) in shaping social attitudes. These declarations may be treated as a certain resistance of respondents in Berlin to propaganda and populist messages.

Students were also asked about their individual attitude expressed with the willingness to share the neighbourhood with immigrants who recently arrived to Europe. Among the students from Berlin, 90% were ready to live in the neighbourhood with immigrants, and among those in Krakow, 33% made such a declaration.

## 4.5 Summary of the Second Stage of Research

Summing up the above survey results, we may point that the main information channels for students in Berlin and Krakow are Internet portals and television. Respondents in Berlin more often read the press while students in Krakow prefer Internet channels. An important source of information concerning the issue of migration is direct communication with family and friends and own experiences (these were mainly indicated by students from Berlin). This confirms that first, students in Berlin are more prone to formulate their own opinions about migration, what follows from their own experiences from living in a multicultural society, while respondents in Krakow much more often in their opinions about migration processes copy arguments heard on television or read on social websites. In the case of information from mass media, it should be remembered that the reception of news is influenced not only by its content but also by the construction of headline, lead and comments that are anonymously added by users on the Internet. Research carried out in Poland in the University of Social Sciences and Humanities by Konrad Maj revealed that it is not the content of a piece of news but the lead or the headline that influences the shaping of individual attitudes. Quite often, the attitude of recipients to news is the result of the fact that a person does not read the content but limits themselves only to the headline or the lead and on this basis shapes their opinion about the content of a particular piece of news. On TV this is the function of the so-called breaking news bar, where brief messages are shown. Second, if an important source of information about migrants is direct communication, it should be supposed that the messages transmitted by family or friends influence the shaping of students' opinions. Thus, the sources of opinion may be also looked for in culturally conditioned messages – the attitude to aliens that follows from dominating cultural patterns in each country.

The survey made at the second stage of research confirmed conclusions from the pilot research concerning the sense of threat connected with the inflow of immigrants. In the survey carried out in 2014, a higher level of anxiety was revealed by students from Poland than from Germany, where the actual contact with representatives of other national or ethnic groups is common. As the main source of anxiety, students from both cities indicated the terrorist threat, which may be treated as justified in the face of terrorist attacks that took place in the EU. Simultaneously, the increased sense of threat among students from Krakow also influences growth of nationalist attitudes, particularly in the context of enhancing it with media messages.

Juxtaposition of the activity of students from Krakow and from Berlin as regards the activities aimed against migrants (participation in protests against migrants and happenings for aiding migrants) revealed a greater engagement of students from Berlin. In Krakow, respondents did not show initiative in protesting against migrants or organising support for them. A bigger engagement of students in Berlin is also manifested in the space of discussion devoted to the issue of migration. In social media, respondents from Berlin more often organised themselves in happenings and organising aid for immigrants in comparison to students from Krakow. Even if the latter of the activities may be treated as premature, because in Poland there is no question of the inflow of immigrants, the problem of migration is discussed in mass media in Poland and research proves that students are not interested in this topic at all.

Interesting research results are presented in an analysis of attitudes to immigrants that were shown by students in each city. The opinions of students in Berlin were much more influenced by the humanitarianism principle, compared to opinions expressed by the respondents in Krakow. Moreover, both groups quite unequivocally admit that the main reason of migration is the will to lead a more comfortable life, but for the respondents in Berlin, this motivation of migrants seems to be rational and legitimate and for the ones from Krakow it is not. Students from Krakow emphasise that migrants should reform their own countries rather than run away from them. In their opinions, the respondents also directly defined their attitude to migrants. And thus, students in Krakow, contrary to their peers from Berlin, believe that migrants will destroy European civilisation and that monocultural countries develop better. The degree of individualisation in perceiving migrants is also lower. At the same time, analysing mechanisms of influencing others used in media messages in order to shape certain attitudes through them, we may state that respondents in both cities did not show significant differences as regards acknowledging the effectiveness of the used techniques.

In the group of respondents in Krakow, about 20% were from Ukraine. The results analysed also contain their answers. In the whole study, we may notice similarity of answers given by Polish and Ukrainian students. There were differences as regards answers to the questions that concerned the attitude to migrants, as in fact students from Ukraine are immigrants in Poland. Ukrainians drew more attention to the necessity of individual treatment of migrants, particularly in the context of their political situation, which is sometimes the cause of migration. They more often also agreed that migrants have the right to a better and more comfortable life, which is the justification for migration and the reason why the accepting country should help such people. Respondents of Ukrainian origin also more often than their Polish friends acknowledged that the presentation of the political situation in the country of origin may be an effective mechanism encouraging to help migrants and their individualisation in the accepting country. In this part of the study, there appeared a self-reflection of students from Ukraine, manifested in waiting for the understanding of their situation in the accepting country, like Poland.

Conclusions from the second stage of research have become the basis for preparing methodology of the last stage of research, the objective of which was establishing to what extent the communication processes on the Internet, particularly in the space of social services, may influence cultural unification, also including the shaping of a similar attitude to immigrants and promoting multiculturalism in countries where this phenomenon is still treated as a social and political challenge.

## 4.6 The Use of Social Media in Communication Processes of Representatives of High- and Low-Context Cultures

The last stage of research concerned the analysis of communication attitudes of students on the Internet, with the subject of interest being the presence of cultural values identified according to the model of cultures by Geert Hofstede – identification of high- and low-context cultures.

It follows from the analysis that 194 people out of the students surveyed in Berlin use the social media, in Krakow 196 people while in Kiev all respondents, i.e. 200 people. The most frequent reason for using the social media according to the respondents' declarations is the access to current information (56.71% of answers in Berlin, 67% in Krakow and 72.5% in Kiev). Similar responses were also given by students to the question about the use of social media for keeping up or building relations on the Internet (48.98% of answers in Berlin, 52.58% in Krakow and 42.5% in Kiev). Social media were regarded as channels that are not important for presenting one's own opinions and views by students in Berlin and Krakow (54.64% of answers in Berlin, 51.54% in Krakow and 29.5% in Kiev). The respondents in Kiev revealed differentiated attitudes in this respect because as many as 45% of the respondents pointed that such channels are an important place as regards the opportunity to present their views and opinions for them. Access to entertainment and fun was indicated as an important possibility by 55.16% of the students in Berlin. For respondents in Krakow and Kiev, this reason was not that important. It was treated as unimportant by as many as 42.86% of the respondents in Krakow and 57.5% in Kiev. On the other hand, the question to what extent the students use the social media to create and share content with other users was chosen as the most important possibility by the respondents from Kiev (53.5% answers). Students from Krakow (25%) and over half of the students from Berlin (54.12%) indicated this value as completely unimportant.

Analysing the presented data, we may state that using social media by students in each city has not so much cultural importance but a political one. The political system in Germany and Poland may be treated as so stable that Internet users are much less engaged in activities aimed at overcoming the deficit of democracy through new media. More often the channels in new media are used as carriers of entertainment and fun, information and the means to keep up relations with other users. Ukraine is in this respect far from political standards of the other two countries. It is a country where there is still a deficit of democratic values, so the Internet is the source of knowledge, information and building Ukrainian identity, particularly for young people. Social media were used widely and on a mass scale during protests at Euromaidan and also at the time when in Ukraine there were no mass media promoting democratic values, what reassured young people (and it was mainly because of them that the events at Maidan took place) that the Internet was an important carrier of information and it enabled showing one's views freely. As regards students from all the studied cities, they thought that the dominating reasons for which they used the social media were access to information and building and keeping up relations with friends.

Students were asked what channels in social media they use the most often. Students' declarations are presented in Table 2.

*Table 2: Channels in social media used by students*

| Channels in social media | Berlin | Krakow | Kiev |
|---|---|---|---|
| Video/content websites | 46.91% | 65.82% | 63.50% |
| Social websites | 62.89% | 79.6% | 78% |
| Blogs | 7.73% | 23.98% | 12% |
| Games | 11.86% | 14.28% | 13.50% |
| Chats and forums | 10.31% | 12.75% | 24% |
| Mobile applications | 36.6% | 30.1% | 39.50% |

Own elaboration.

Results in all of the above categories revealed similar preferences in the choice of the used social media. Data presented in Table 2 show that social websites, like Facebook, Twitter, Instagram and Snapchat (in Kiev, students also declared using the VKontakte website), are most popular in all three cities. Students in all three cities equally often use mobile applications and content websites, like YouTube and Vimeo. Students in Kiev much more often than their peers in Krakow and Berlin declared using forums and chats. This confirms the data analysed above, in which students in Kiev more often declared that in network communication they present their own opinions and views. On the other hand, respondents in Krakow more often than their friends in Berlin and Kiev read blogs as carriers of content. It may be because blogs have become quite fashionable in Poland, both as regards keeping one's own blogs and reading those kept by other users, particularly celebrities, but it is also a manifestation of individualism that is articulated in the content of blogs.

Another research issue was the analysis of network activity of students concerning publication of materials (like posts, films and photos) on social networks that present other cultural values than the ones shared by them and that stem from the culture they have grown up in.

*Table 3: Different cultural content in social media*

| Content in social media | Berlin | Krakow | Kiev |
|---|---|---|---|
| Yes, I publish content presenting other cultural values | 21.35% | 30.11% | 50% |
| I do not publish content presenting other cultural values | 50% | 32.65% | 22.61% |
| I do not pay attention to it | 28.65% | 37.24% | 27.14% |

Own elaboration.

Analysing the data presented in Table 3, we may state that students both in Krakow and in Kiev, other than their friends from Berlin, use social media to promote content that is culturally different than their own. This may result from the fact that students in Krakow and Kiev treat differences as something unique and at the same time interesting. On the other hand, as was found in the pilot study of 2014, students in Berlin have everyday contacts with representatives of other cultures, which automatically means that they do not treat communication on the Internet as a place where it is interesting to share content referring to different cultural values. Students experience them on a daily basis. However, the data emphasise that for the respondents in Krakow and Kiev social media are an important channel through which they get to know and share content about multiculturalism. This may confirm the deficit of such experiences in everyday life of the respondents.

Students were also asked if they hold conversations about political issues on the social media channels they use. Answers given by respondents confirmed that in all three cities students are rather not interested in such issues. In Berlin 28.13% of respondents reacted positively, in Krakow 29.08%, and in Kiev 18.59%. A lower index of positive answers in Kiev may be due to the fact that in recent years political situation has been the subject of increased interest of Internet users, what led to a kind of reluctance to tackle this subject and to look for other issues in social media.

The study also aimed to find out the role of the Internet as a source of information published in mass media, i.e. the press. The respondents were asked if they read electronic versions of newspapers through the Internet and if they share links to interesting articles through social websites. Also in this case students' answers were similar: 57.81% of students in Berlin, 62.76%

in Krakow and 61.11% in Kiev declared themselves as readers of electronic versions of newspapers sharing links further on their social websites. Students' answers to the question about commenting the content of articles to which they published links on social websites also looked similar (35.83% of answers in Berlin, 41.5% in Krakow and 41.09% in Kiev). The responses also confirmed a similar attitude of students towards content published by them on the Internet – they share it more often than they comment on it. Similarity of attitudes towards content disseminated by the respondents was also shown by friends of the respondents – commenting on published articles was declared more often (61.54% of answers in Berlin, 65.57% in Krakow and 57% in Kiev). These data prove that network communication behaviour of users is the same, regardless of the type of culture represented by them.

Another research issue was the analysis of the content of articles that the respondents share most often.

*Table 4: Content shared by students on their social websites*

| Article topics | Berlin | Krakow | Kiev |
|---|---|---|---|
| Politics | 56.82% | 22.58% | 18.70% |
| History | 9.2% | 22.58% | 26.37% |
| Religion | 12.65% | 22.58% | 22.33% |
| Social issues | 68.96% | 30.65% | 48.21% |
| Multiculturalism | 34.09% | 30.65% | 32% |
| Satire and jokes | 52.27% | 57.26% | 50.46% |
| Patriotic and national content | 2.3% | 16.13% | 43.12% |
| Information about scandals | 13.79% | 14.51% | 21.10% |
| Educational content | 36.37% | 33.06% | 55.45% |
| Development of new technologies | 18.39% | 32.26% | 28% |
| Globalisation and migration | 34.09% | 17.76% | 19% |

Own elaboration.

Table 4 shows the topics of articles that the respondents most often shared on their own social websites. Answers given by students in three cities present cultural differences (understood in the light of a high- and low-context culture) that result from the content of issues shared on the Internet. And thus students in Berlin (as representatives of a low-context culture) share information concerning politics (which does not simultaneously mean that they comment on it or talk about it), but issues connected with religion, patriotism and history are not interesting for them. For students in Berlin, social issues and topics connected with globalisation and migrations are also important. For respondents from Kiev (as representatives of a high-context culture), on the other hand, topics connected with history and religion are important, as well as patriotic and national issues (which may mainly stem from the shaping of the Ukrainian identity noted after the events at Euromaidan). Another important type of content that the respondents from Kiev share on the Internet are issues connected with education. Explanation for the use of the Internet in educational processes should rather be found in the students' search for knowledge alternative to the one offered by the Ukrainian educational system. In Berlin and in Krakow using the Internet in educational activities is normal. The issues of migrations and globalisation that take place in the world to a much lesser extent arouse interest of people in Krakow and Kiev, which may result from the fact that in both of these cities this issue is not an identifiable problem that directly concerns the respondents.

Continuing the topic of analysis of shared cultural values, students were asked about advertising message concerning their country that they would share in the used social services. Table 5 presents the results.

*Table 5: Values declared by students in shared advertising messages*

| Content of advertising message | Berlin | Krakow | Kiev |
|---|---|---|---|
| Ironically treating the country's history | 26.96% | 8.67% | 5.03% |
| Presenting the most important values for the country's inhabitants | 13.48% | 28.07% | 36.68% |
| Ridiculing national vices of fellow countrymen | 35.96% | 7.65% | 0 |
| Describing the beauty of homeland | 23.60% | 55.61% | 58.29 |

Own elaboration.

As follows from the data presented in Table 5, students differ as to the declared content that they would share on a social website as an advertising message promoting their homeland. Respondents in Berlin, as representatives of a low-context culture, where individualistic values dominate, are more divided in their preferences as to the propagated advertising message about their country. They also allow publicising such materials that would ironically refer to the presentation of history of their country (26.96%)

or would ridicule national vices of their fellow countrymen (35.96%). Attitudes of students in Krakow and Kiev are much less varied, both groups present rather collectivist values that minimise individualism and promote thinking about the group. Students in Krakow and Kiev are rather prone to share information that describe their country only in positive terms on social websites – presenting values that are shared by the inhabitants of the country as a group and describing the beauty of the country.

Another research issue was the analysis of use of social websites for self-presentation purposes, i.e. promoting the achieved success and boasting about it. It turned out that 56.12% of students from Krakow and 44.44% from Kiev do it; in Berlin using social media for this purpose was declared by 32.47% of respondents. The identified differences may be the result of cultural differences – an individualistic or collectivist culture, where individuals have different relations with the group, e.g. rooted in the attitude to rivalry. However, taking into account that simultaneously with the representation of different cultures there occurs the phenomenon of a varied level of economic development, differences in presenting achievements (in the study, it was not precisely stated what kind of success this exactly concerned) may also be an illustration of those with mainly economic meaning, which in the society with dominating values encouraging free expression (Germany) are less important than in the societies where values still promote survival (Ukraine and Poland).

Interactions the individuals enter into in network communication were analysed in the study. Students were asked about their attitudes to different situations that identify interpersonal relations on the Internet.

*Table 6: Interactions the students get into with people who do not share their views*

| Quarrelling in Internet discussions | Berlin | Krakow | Kiev |
|---|---|---|---|
| Yes | 19.69% | 30.61% | 50% |
| No | 80.31% | 69.39% | 50% |

Own elaboration.

The results presented in Table 6 illustrate the tendency to quarrel on the Internet, which does not seem to be a derivative of a culture represented by the respondents. Half of the students in Kiev, as the representatives of a collectivist culture, where entering into direct confrontations is frowned upon, declared that they enter such relations as quarrels when they participate in discussions on the Internet. On the other hand, students in Berlin, as representatives of an individualistic culture, show a smaller propensity for quarrels and confrontational way of discussing things on the Internet. The analysis of data presented in Table 6 may also be considered in the context of juxtaposing it with the criterion of masculinity. Social role of gender creates differences between ways of solving conflicts. In "feminine" countries, conflicts are resolved through compromise and negotiations; in "masculine" countries, verbal fights are held. Ukraine, according to the criterion proposed by Geert Hofstede, represents a model of culture with a low level of masculinisation, contrary to Germany or Poland. Research, the results of which have been presented above, shows the level of aggression in network discussions, with an opposite distribution to the level of "masculinity" of the analysed communities. Looking for a justification other than the cultural indexes, we may find the explanation in the fact that in Ukraine an intensive process of political changes has been going on for a few years and it has influenced the identity-shaping process. This may be important for network communication, where users, differing in opinions, freely use the freedom of expression and hold disputes about their views.

*Table 7: Effects of differing in discussions*

| Removing people with different views from friends | Berlin | Krakow | Kiev |
|---|---|---|---|
| Yes | 42.41% | 24.49% | 27.78% |
| No | 57.59% | 75.51% | 72.22% |

Own elaboration.

Table 7 shows declared students' attitudes to cultural differences revealed in network conversations. Respondents in Berlin are more prone to remove people who have different views than their own from their circle of friends. Students from Berlin, as representatives of an individualistic culture, have loose relations with other people, value harmony and voluntariness of interactions, and are reluctant to confront views other than their own. However, responses given by students in Krakow were quite interesting. They rather represent an individualistic culture according to the model by Geert Hofstede, but the attitudes revealed in the study were closer to those presented by their counterparts from Kiev, as representatives of a collectivist culture. This may indicate that students from Krakow do not share values characteristic of the model of an individualistic culture, or being also representatives of a highly masculine culture, they are interested in having people representing other cultural values in their circle of friends, with whom it is possible to talk, also as adversaries (Table 6 revealed a relatively high level of aggression shown by Polish students who quarrel on the Internet).

*Table 8: Overcoming gender schemas*

| A woman as the person initiating contact with a strange man on Facebook | Berlin | Krakow | Kiev |
|---|---|---|---|
| Yes | 77.37% | 83.16% | 52.02% |
| No | 20.53% | 9.69% | 23.23% |
| It may be taken in the wrong way | 2.11% | 7.15% | 24.75% |

Own elaboration.

Table 8 illustrates attitudes of students that they adopt in connection with overcoming the schema of gender. The survey has revealed that students from Kiev are the most strongly burdened with a stereotype of a woman who should not initiate contacts with male strangers on a social website because it might be taken the wrong way. Students from Krakow are the most liberal as regards overcoming barriers resulting from the gender schema in starting network relations, among which the largest number of people points to such behaviour as being acceptable. It seems that following the criterion of uncertainty avoidance identified by Hofstede, we may assume that Ukrainian students have clearly defined principles of what is allowed and what is not, in order to avoid uncertainty. On the other hand, analysing these results in the context of the individualism and collectivism criterion, we may state that students in Kiev, as representatives of a high-context culture, where collective culture dominates, believe that women should be chaste and starting relations on the Internet with strange men is a breach of this principle and it may be taken the wrong way.

*Table 9: Revealing own views in network discussion*

| Anxiety/fear of revealing own views when commenting on other users' posts | Berlin | Krakow | Kiev |
|---|---|---|---|
| Yes | 55.26% | 31.63% | 28.79% |
| No | 44.74% | 68.37% | 71.21% |

Own elaboration.

Table 9 illustrating the level of anxiety of students about revealing and presenting one's own views in Internet discussions, different than the content of posts that they comment on, shows the highest level of anxiety in students in Berlin. It seems that the data presented in the table should be analysed in the context of the phenomenon of political correctness that prevents frank articulation of views in network communication, where comments do not have a private character and their content is visible to other users. Although students from Berlin represent an individualistic culture, openness in speaking their mind is for them limited in the public space. Political correctness as a social phenomenon is not that strong in Poland and in Ukraine, which is also confirmed by students declaring bigger openness to commenting on content with which they do not agree, thus revealing their own views. Data presented in Table 9 may also be juxtaposed with results of previous analyses. Students in Kiev and Krakow hold open disputes on the Internet, also quarrelling, they are not prone to remove friends who do not share their views and opinions and who express differences having cultural sources. Such attitudes may be the effect of lack of political correctness in respondents in Krakow and Kiev, and thus create a potential possibility of a more open discussion.

*Table 10: Revealing religious beliefs in network discussions*

| Treating social media as a place for revealing religious beliefs | Berlin | Krakow | Kiev |
|---|---|---|---|
| Yes | 34.38% | 34.18% | 14.65% |
| No | 65.63% | 65.82% | 85.35% |

Own elaboration.

Students declared different views concerning revealing their own religious beliefs on the Internet (Table 10). Students in Berlin and Krakow have a similar attitude in this respect, while the vast majority of students in Kiev think that social media are not a good place where one's own religious beliefs should be presented. These data are surprising, considering the fact that over 70% of students in Kiev at the same time stated that social media are a place for them where they can present their opinions and views. Justification for such answers obtained in Kiev should rather be looked for in the age of the respondents and the use of social media to reduce deficits.

*Table 11: Sharing information on the Internet at the request of virtual friends*

| Sharing information we do not agree with on the Internet at the request of friends | Berlin | Krakow | Kiev |
|---|---|---|---|
| Yes | 2.59% | 5.61% | 16.24% |
| No | 97.41% | 94.39% | 83.76% |

Own elaboration.

Table 11 illustrates the attitude of students to sharing information on the Internet that was published by their friends asking the respondents to share it further. But the respondents do not agree with the content of information itself. According to the students' declarations, in Berlin they are the least prone to share such information while in Kiev they do it much more often, which means that they are less assertive to the requests of virtual friends. These attitudes confirm values characteristic of a low-context culture (Germany) and a high-context culture (Ukraine), as regards the individualism criterion. In a collective culture that the students from Ukraine represent, a desirable feature is loyalty to the group, which in this particular case is manifested in sharing content that the respondents themselves do not support, but it is important for members of the virtual community they belong to (their Internet friends). This is contrary to the individualist culture represented by German students, where valued features include voluntariness of relations and honesty to others.

*Table 12: Imitation on the Internet*

| Imitating friends in liking posts on Facebook | Berlin | Krakow | Kiev |
|---|---|---|---|
| Yes | 1.04% | 3.06% | 6.57% |
| No | 50.26% | 58.16% | 85.86% |
| If I agree with the content | 48.7% | 38.78% | 7.58% |

Own elaboration.

Imitation as an attitude is more often found in Ukrainian than in German students (Table 12). Respondents in Kiev, as representatives of a collective culture, are more prone to express an attitude pointing to membership in a group and behaviour similar to other representatives of one's own group than respondents in Berlin or Krakow. At the same time, Ukrainian students much more often than their German or Polish peers declare that they are not interested in acting similar to other representatives of the same group. This may mean that they negate collectivism but at the same time do not take individual decisions, in this case making the decision dependent on supporting the content. The respondents in Berlin and in Krakow, with their declarations, confirmed that they are members of an individualist culture.

Another research problem was the attempt to analyse activity of students in computer games and their attitude to using social networks for such activities.

*Table 13: Activity of students in computer games*

| Students' declarations concerning the use of computer games | Berlin | Krakow | Kiev |
|---|---|---|---|
| Yes | 41.15% | 35.71% | 39.39% |
| No | 58.85% | 64.29% | 60.61% |

Own elaboration.

Data presented in Table 13 are an exemplification of one of the reasons for which students use social media. For respondents from Berlin, entertainment and fun provided by social media are important. This is shown in Table 13 informing that students in Berlin are the most active as regards using computer games. Answering this question, the respondents in Krakow and Kiev confirmed earlier declarations defining reasons for which they use social media. Entertainment and fun are not important motivations for them.

*Table 14: Students' attitudes concerning the opinion of their parents about games they use*

| Acceptance of the chosen games by parents | Berlin | Krakow | Kiev |
|---|---|---|---|
| Yes | 9.52% | 2.86% | 13.87% |
| No | 17.86% | 31.43% | 27.17% |
| I am not interested in it | 72.62% | 65.71% | 58.96% |

Own elaboration.

The analysis shown in Table 14 was aimed at proving to what extent students share power distance (understood as parents' power) in network communication. The study, although it was carried out among adults, revealed that respondents, albeit to a different degree, declare dependence on the opinion of their own parents. Ukrainian students, as representatives of a high power distance culture, are simultaneously more prone to respect their parents' opinion concerning the choice of games they play. Different attitudes are represented by students in Krakow and Berlin, where definitely the largest group declared lack of interest in their parents' opinions, which would confirm the existence of a low power distance.

Students were also asked about the most important criteria for them in choosing games that they play in their free time.

*Table 15: Students' declarations concerning the criteria of choosing computer games*

| Criteria of choosing computer games | Berlin | Krakow | Kiev |
|---|---|---|---|
| Graphic attractiveness | 55.72% | 44.74% | 50.44% |
| Theme | 81.09% | 84.21% | 76.31% |
| Difficulty | 24.29% | 32.89% | 46.49% |
| Popularity | 11.76% | 22.37% | 41.07% |
| Used cultural symbols | 8.82% | 7.9% | 16.03% |
| Recommendations of virtual friends | 10.29% | 26.32% | 31.58% |

Own elaboration.

As follows from Table 15, students' declarations concerning criteria they use to choose computer games are varied. The main factor in choosing a game is its theme and attractiveness. The used cultural symbols are not an important selection criterion – a relatively higher score of this criterion in Kiev may prove the enhancement of the national identity, which is reflected in the topic of the game through relevant cultural symbols. For students from Berlin, such elements as recommending the game by friends (high level of individualism) and its popularity are not very important, which is contrary to students from Kiev for whom these elements are important for choosing the used game. These answers by students in Kiev should be treated as proving the existence of collective values.

The respondents were also asked which holidays are celebrated by them. This question was not significant for communication processes that take place on the Internet, but it was important for the presentation of students' attitudes in real reality, as regards their attitude to their own culture and its dominating values.

*Table 16: Students' declarations concerning celebrated holidays*

| Celebrating holidays by students | Berlin | Krakow | Kiev |
|---|---|---|---|
| Yes | 43.81% | 77.05% | 77% |
| No | 32.47% | 12.24% | 7% |
| Only religious holidays | 17.53% | 8.16% | 7% |
| Only national holidays | 6.19% | 2.55% | 9% |

Own elaboration.

Table 16 presents different attitudes of students from Berlin, at the same time emphasising the dominating individualism and the resulting right of the individual to choose. On the other hand, respondents in Krakow and Kiev revealed similar attitudes as regards celebrated holidays. For both groups, it is important to celebrate holidays in general, although students in Krakow more often declared not celebrating holidays at all. On the other hand, respondents in Kiev more often declared celebrating national holidays, which should rather be explained with the growing sense of national identity.

## 4.7 Summary of the Third Stage of Research

The respondents have shown different attitudes in connection with using the social media. Everybody uses them mainly to access current information and keep up or build relations with friends. Students in Berlin treat social media as the source of fun and entertainment, more often than their Ukrainian friends. On the other hand, respondents in Kiev put much more attention to the possibility of presentation of their own opinions and views on the Internet and the chance to create and share their own content. Differences in these attitudes should rather be looked for in the political and social situation of the respondents. Students in Kiev for a few years have taken part in the processes of shaping the national identity, which was manifested during protests at Maidan at the turn of the 2013 and 2014, initiated by young people. Moreover, Ukrainian students intensively used the social media as communication channels during protests, creating alternative content to the news presented in Ukrainian mass media, thus revealing their own views and opinions about the changing political and social reality. Looking for a reference to cultural differences identified by Geert Hofstede, we may conclude that German students, as representatives of the individualistic culture, are more focused on satisfying their own needs than on building a network community in the processes of communication. Creating a community may in this case mean being active in social media, that is designing one's own content and sharing it, at the same time identifying and disseminating one's own views.

Respondents in all three cities declared using the same channels in social media. Students in Kiev use chats and forums more often than their counterparts from other cities, which would confirm previous findings about bigger engagement in the area of presenting one's own opinions and views on the Internet. For students in Kiev, social media are a place of popularising content presenting different cultural values, which may also mean that the respondents find on the Internet the information that they are not able to obtain from other sources. It is interesting information for them that they pay attention to and notice the cultural dissimilarity, with their source in Internet news. Research revealed that preferences of students concerning the choice of channels in social media and communication behaviour on the Internet are similar, regardless of the cultural model the students belong to. Respondents are more willing to share information on the Internet than comment on them. Also, the users who are engaged in playing computer games declared, regardless of the type of culture that they represent, that it is the theme and attractiveness of games that is the criterion of choice of a particular game by them.

Cultural differences are distinctly visible in students as regards the thematic scope of content that they promote on the Internet. German students clearly demonstrate that they belong to a culture where individualistic values dominate and which is orientated on the future, by showing that the topics concerning history, religion, patriotism and national values were much less important for them. But important issues include politics, globalisation, migrations, and social matters. For students from Kiev, as representatives of a collectivist culture, important topics are those regarded as quite unimportant by their German counterparts. Students from all studied cities chose satirical and jocular comments about reality as the most important content for them. This would confirm that network communication is less formal and it enables more humorous comments about reality than in media regarded as traditional channels of communication. Sharing satirical messages by students is explained by the global phenomenon of memes, which usually comment on the reality in a jocular manner. However, it should be emphasised here that interest in looking for satirical and humorous content alone does not mean that for all respondents the same jokes are acceptable. This results from distinct cultural differences that were shown in students' declarations concerning the advertising message about their country that they would share on social websites. The respondents in Germany, as representatives of a culture with a low power distance, not only had differing opinions but in over half of the answers allowed ironic content and ridiculing national vices of their compatriots as these materials that they would be able to publish. Students from Krakow and Kiev confirmed that in this respect they shared values characteristic of a culture with a higher power distance index.

Analysing the declared activity of students in social media, it should be emphasised that it presents strong influence of cultural values on attitudes and behaviour of students, particularly in the context of identification of individualistic and collectivist cultures. Such attitudes are noticeable in the answers of Polish students who sometimes are somewhere between the representatives of individualistic and collectivist culture but more often show features of the former. However, attention should be drawn to the fact that more often it is the representatives of collectivist cultures who tend to show individualistic features in network communication processes than the other way round. This enables putting forward a hypothesis that social media may in the long run influence the increase of the level of individualisation of attitudes of individuals, simultaneously leaving from the model of a collectivist culture to the individualistic one, not only as regards attitudes revealed in virtual reality but also sharing cultural values. More often it is also Ukrainian students who treat the topics published on the Internet as a potential source of education and thus in the long run the reason of potential cultural changes, than students in Berlin. It is interesting and important in the context of analysis of previous research to establish that German students are much more anxious to reveal their own views on the Internet than their counterparts from Krakow and Kiev (also as regards presenting opinions and views on the Internet, students in Berlin showed much less interest). It seems that the influence on the reluctance of students in Berlin to manifest their own views and to comment on posts of other users is exerted by political correctness, which introduces a dissonance between what the student would want to show and what they really think, and this what is the limitation of their freedom of speech in the context of political correctness and participation in public debates. Another possible explanation would be the higher level of awareness of consequences among students in Berlin, which is manifested in greater caution in expressing views and opinions on the Internet, what in fact also boils down to acknowledging the existence of political correctness as a category standardising social relations.

To sum up, the above research presented a dependence of content shown on the Internet on sharing certain cultural values by students, which usually results from the fact of socialisation going in accordance with defined dominating cultural patterns. Despite the fact that attitudes and communication behaviour are similar, the message itself depends on the cultural model shared by the student. The most important criterion that determines differences in content published on the Internet depends on the type of collectivist and individualistic culture. And it is possible to observe that students from collectivist cultures show tendencies to individualistic attitudes in network communication and not the other way round. This leads to a conclusion that communication with the use of channels in social media may lead to increasing individualisation of attitudes, which, as a result, may modify cultural identities of an individual.

# Network Communication and Cultural Identity of an Individual – Summary Attempt

In the reality where forms of real and virtual communication intertwine, nobody is surprised by the popularity of channels in social media, which are more and more popular forms of communication between individuals [Sawyer 2011]. Younger network users do not look for confirmation or verification of network information in the mass media anymore. For them, the content in new media is an autonomous source of information which satisfies their needs. Network communication is also becoming a form of promoting intercultural communication, which, on the one hand, results from the ease of exchanging information through new media and the availability of participation in the exchange. On the other hand, it facilitates connecting people in loose but numerous interactions, on many levels. Research carried out so far presents the complexity of processes of exchange of information that occurs, thanks to network communication, emphasising more and more often its significance for supporting intercultural communication, also in the global sense [Allwood, Schroeder 2000; Veltri, Elgarah 2009; Vasslou, Joinson, Coourvoisier 2010; Vinuales 2011; Chen 2012]. What is more, we may assume that more and more often cultural axioms influence processes of network communication. This monograph is part of the trend of research into cultural differences in the context of network communication processes and the role of social media in cultural changes that occur in the globalised world. The way of carrying out the research has made it possible to show cultural differences in a way presenting their sources identified in communication attitudes and behaviour of users. At the same time, the research carried out in stages made it possible to verify research conclusions gradually during consecutive analyses.

In the part devoted to theoretical considerations on multiculturalism and political cosmopolitanism, research results proved that age is an important criterion as regards positive attitude to the very phenomenon of cosmopolitanism. Over 20% of young people share ideas accompanying the justification of cosmopolitanism as an alternative for reproducing social inequalities resulting from belonging to a certain social group. On the

Internet, which is a place where there is no obligation to explicitly define oneself, it is possible to end the relationship at any time because it is usually liquid and unstable but, on the other hand, it is also possible to promote one's own views, supporting the shared values. The Internet is becoming a space where individuals identify their identity, at the same time looking for justification for its enhancement or change. The Internet supports and identifies individualism, shapes new identities based on culture and participation, which virtual relations not only make possible but also enhance, often transferring the effects into real reality. Intercultural communication, particularly among the students who do not have their own experiences being the result of living in a multicultural environment, is becoming the subject of interest in network relations and the respondents in Poland and Ukraine, having their own cultural roots, in the space of social media look for values that would enrich their cultural system, particularly in the context of providing knowledge that is unavailable in traditional media. Network communication from the time perspective may be important in enhancing multiculturalism in the leftist-liberal meaning (McLaren's typology – author's remark), blurring cultural differences and appealing to universal humanism in promoting values. Another possible effect in the context of using social websites for promoting multiculturalism is the development of critical multiculturalism, which assumes promoting diversity, what may also evoke curiosity, interest and at the same time the desire to know. Alien cultural forms are more and more often subject to reception in accordance with local rules, in specific communities, where they are interpreted not according to cultural patterns of a national nature but with patterns adopted by these communities, based on their own experiences, also resulting from cultural contact. Such cultural contact that takes place in network communication and shows differences resulting from cultural differences at the same time shows how these differences are levelled by diminishing the authority of family which is the basic carrier of cultural content (regardless of the type of culture – collective or individualistic). The effects of the phenomenon of levelling the differences are particularly visible in reactions of young people belonging to societies presenting values of a high-context culture. Peer relations are becoming more important than the authority of the family, leading to the situation that contact with a different culture for younger users is becoming not so much the source of anxiety but inspiration and interest.

On the Internet, users often identify their attitudes guided by universal humanism, which triggers imitation as the way of network activity. Geert Hofstede noticed that overcoming cultural divides is more difficult in collective than in individualist societies. At the same time, however, network communication supports individualism of the individual, which leads to the situation that they enter into relations characteristic of individualist culture, gradually modifying their own cultural paradigms. We may thus forecast that the "political race" as the scientific proposal of a political and social solution will find its source of promotion in network communication, in messages appealing to universal humanism and promoting diversity as the basis of development and not only threat.

A separate research issue that appeared in the context of analysis of results obtained in the course of research is the problem of dealing with stereotypes. Individuals do not want to admit that their attitudes and behaviour are guided by stereotypes. Political correctness as a model of behaviour dictates automatic overcoming of stereotypes, which leads to the phenomenon of modern racism, where the individual is actually prejudiced, but for social reasons they do not reveal it on the outside. Research has shown that some respondents (this phenomenon has been more strongly reported in the analysis of network behaviour manifested by German students) define their attitudes revealed in network communication as accepting diversity, declaring support for migration, at the same time presenting a significant level of anxiety for revealing their true opinions online, more often also declaring removal from their circle of friends – people who do not share the same cultural values as the respondent. We may assume that not only the content presented by the respondents on the Internet but also the analysis of attitudes presented in communication behaviour give meaning to cultural values. It follows from the declarations of students from Berlin that they actually did not take part in the events that in real reality were connected with protests against migration but 54.5% of respondents personally know people who took part in such events.

Attitudes observed in virtual reality do not always result only from belonging to a high- or low-context culture. Collective behaviour of Germans revealed on the Internet concerning migrants should rather be treated as a manifestation of maturity of the civil society, which is guided by the principle of humanism and empathy, levelling discriminative behaviour, even if some users are guided by concealed racism. Modern racism is stereotypical thinking that is hidden behind political correctness. Such racism is manifested in the fact that declarations accepting sharing common space with migrants are not accompanied by actual actions to improve the fate of people who found themselves in the accepting country. Such conclusions have been formulated on the basis of the analysis of attitudes declared by German students, over 80% of which regarded the inflow of migrants to Europe as a positive phenomenon, but only a little over 20% were in any way engaged in helping them.

Polish students, on the other hand, showing a considerable lack of empathy to migrants and insecurity in the economic sense, rather proved the weakness of civil society in Poland. However, it is futile to justify the deficit of civil attitudes in Poland only with cultural values; it is rather a consequence of political and social heritage. Discrimination of migrants revealed in the attitudes of Polish students is the source of prejudice, the effects of which may be looked for in the lack of empathy. This conclusion follows from analyses of opinions of students about the causes of migration and manifestations of competition for economic goods in threats that are brought by the inflow of migrants to Europe. Moreover, analysing current attitudes defined and presented in the mass media in Poland, we may assume that discrimination is institutional in nature. There is a conformist assent to racist or xenophobic statements that come from people who have influence on shaping public opinion, including politicians. The mass media provide cultural values dominating in the society. In Poland, mainly because the idea of multiculturalism is not allowed in public space, these values are only national in nature, actually promoting nationalist ideas. On the other hand, new media, in particular social websites, are an alternative space where young users look for different content or have the possibility to obtain information of different nature than promoting the ethnocentric idea. Moreover, social media shape the educational need, justifying the creation of participative social capital through promoting different cultural values than those to which the mass media refer. According to Jerzy Nikitorowicz, Poland needs new educational strategies that will be adequate to shaping cultural attitudes and competences. This results from the fact that cultural differences are becoming more and more common [Nikitorowicz 2000: 37]. The same author in his text of 2012 remarked that culture that shapes human identity does not catch up with development, including technological development. He writes that in a situation when a person cannot operate culture adequate to the civilisational level there occurs the threat of neo-primitivism, manifested in the lack of respect for humanitarian values in behaviours ignoring social norms [Nikitorowicz 2012: 107]. It seems that the thesis about shortages of social competences and lack of cultural capital in contemporary Poland rather adequately describes the reality and taking into account in this description also the share of the mass media (in escalating xenophobic and nationalist behaviour), the situation is becoming more and more tense in some countries. This diagnosis is also confirmed by Ewa Golebiowska identifying and describing deficits in tolerance and striving to enhance diversity in Poland [Golebiowska 2014].

Also current political issues are important for attitudes revealed online and they may strongly influence communicational behaviour and shape a different cultural identity. Such attitudes could be observed as regards the analysed cultural behaviours of Ukrainian students, where network communication during the events at Euromaidan initiated their strong national identification, which was mainly manifested in activities carried out on the Internet.

The results of research confirmed that the Internet, as a communication channel, enables free participation of individuals in a global exchange, also cultural one. Today, nobody is surprised by celebrities with their own fans who observe their activity mainly on social websites, regardless of the place of residence and actual cultural association. Such a virtue is also attributed to programmes or films that are distributed with the use of the Internet, and for a few years also to computer games, whose fans value most the attractiveness and theme of the game and not cultural values, which the game promotes, or to which it appeals.

Network communication creates new cultural universes based on network channels that are used on a global scale – the most vivid examples seem to be Facebook, YouTube or Google search engine – but also the form of transmitting messages, which include satire and jokes (rather the form), which carry the message of ridiculing the reality. The content itself may not be treated as a universe, as it is still culturally marked, in particular religiously. But using the popular form, it is not difficult to promote with it such cultural messages that will be able to appeal to the educational need of users, thus influencing cultural attitudes.

To sum up the above considerations, this monograph is another confirmation of the significance of the Internet as a place where cultural values of individuals are modified. Attitudes of students taking part in the study are similar in communication activities – they use similar channels in social media, they use them for similar activities and the differences stem from the published themes. And they do not always directly have a culturally conditioned nature, as political or social issues determining messages formulated online are also important. Research confirmed that for students network communication is an important place where communication processes take place, the exchange is going on and relations with others are built. Also in the area of new media, there occur communication processes that are the response to current matters that are not the subject of interest of the mass media, which, as the respondents themselves declare, they even sometimes do not use (the exception is television). Network communication, creating an alternative platform for holding discussions, is becoming not only a place of identification of the identity of the respondents, but also the area where self-reflection and modification of cultural identity becomes possible.

# References

Abbas, T. (2011). Islamic Radicalism and Multicultural Politics: The British Experience. Routledge, Abingdon.

Allport G.W. (1954). *The Nature of Prejudice*. Addison-Wesley Publishing Company, Boston.

Allwood J., Schroeder R. (2000). Intercultural Communication in a Virtual Environment. *Intercultural Communication*, 4.

Arango J. (2010). Explaining migration. A critical view. In S. Vertovec [ed.] *Migration*. Routledge, London and New York.

Archibugi D. (2003). *Debating Cosmopolitics*. Verso, London.

Aronson E., Wilson T.D., Akert R.M. (2006). *Psychologia społeczna* [*Social Psychology*]. Wydawnictwo Zysk i Spółka, Poznań.

Azran T.S. (2016). *Intercultural Communication as a Clash of Civilization. Al Jazeera and Qatar's Soft Power*. Peter Lang Publishing, New York.

Babiński G. (1998). Etniczność [Ethnicity]. In W. Kwaśniewicz [ed.] *Encyklopedia socjologii* [*Encyclopedia of Sociology*]. T. 1. Oficyna Naukowa, Warszawa.

Bagguley, P., Hussain, Y. (2008). Riotous Citizens: Ethnic Conflict in Multicultural Britain. Ashgate, Aldershot.

Bailey O.G., Cammaerts B., Carpentier N. (2012). *Media alternatywne* [*Understanding Alternative Media*]. Wydawnictwo Uniwersytetu Jagiellońskiego, Kraków.

Balawajder E. (2007). Demokracja w świecie wartości [Democracy in the world of values]. In E. Balawajder [ed.] *Społeczeństwo obywatelskie* [*Civil Society*]. Wydawnictwo Katolickiego Uniwersytetu Lubelskiego, Lublin.

Barney D. (2008). *Społeczeństwo sieci* [*The Network Society*]. Wydawnictwo Sic, Warszawa.

Bauman Z. (2003). *Razem osobno* [*Liquid Love: On the Frailty of Human Bonds*]. Wydawnictwo Literackie, Kraków.

Bauman Z. (2006). *Społeczeństwo w stanie oblężenia* [*Society under Siege*]. Wydawnictwo Sic, Warszawa.

Beck U. (2002). *Społeczeństwo ryzyka* [*Risk Society*]. Wydawnictwo Naukowe Scholar, Warszawa.

Beck U., Beck-Gernsheim E. (2013). *Miłość na odległość. Modele życia w epoce globalnej* [*Distant Love*]. Wydawnictwo Naukowe PWN, Warszawa.

Beck U., Giddens A., Lash S. (2009). *Modernizacja refleksyjna* [*Reflexive Modernisation*]. Wydawnictwo Naukowe PWN, Warszawa.

Beck U., Grande E. (2009). *Europa kosmopolityczna. Społeczeństwo i polityka w drugiej nowoczesności* [*Cosmopolitan Europe*]. Wydawnictwo Naukowe Scholar, Warszawa.

Bełkot A. (2016). Model kodowania i dekodowania Stuarta Halla w teoriach komunikacji [Stuart Hall's Encoding/Decoding Model in Communication Theories]. *SenSuS HiStoriae*, 24, 57–79.

Benedict R. (2002). *Wzory kultury* [*Patterns of Culture*]. Warszawskie Wydawnictwo Literackie Muza SA, Warszawa.

Berting J., Villain-Gandossi C. (1995). Rola i znaczenie stereotypów narodowych w stosunkach międzynarodowych. Podejście interdyscyplinarne [The role of stereotypes in international relations]. In T. Walas [ed.] Narody i stereotypy [*Nations and Stereotypes*]. Międzynarodowe Centrum Kultury, Kraków.

Boćwińska-Kiluk B. (2014). Uwarunkowania komunikacji międzykulturowej [Conditions of intercultural communication]. In J. Nikitorowicz, J. Muszyńska, B. Boćwińska-Kiluk [eds.] *Od wielokulturowości miejsca do międzykulturowości relacji społecznych. Współczesne strategie kreowania przestrzeni życia jednostki* [*From Multiculturalism of a Place to Inter-culturalism of Social Relations*]. Wydawnictwo Akademickie Żak, Warszawa.

Bokszański Z. (2006). *Tożsamości zbiorowe* [*Collective Identities*]. Wydawnictwo Naukowe PWN, Warszawa.

Boski P. (2010). *Kulturowe ramy zachowań społecznych* [*Cultural Frameworks of Social Behaviour*]. Wydawnictwo Naukowe PWN, Warszawa.

Bourdieu P., Wacquant L. (2001). *Zaproszenie do socjologii refleksyjnej* [*An Invitation to Reflexive Sociology*]. Oficyna Naukowa, Warszawa.

Brembeck H. (2008). Mediating lifestyles: Food in the file of Bosnian refugee families in Sweden. In K. Romaniszyn [ed.] *Culture and Migration.*

*The Cultural Implications of International Migrations in the Light of Fieldwork Evidence*. Wydawnictwo Nomos, Kraków.

Bursztа W.J. (1998). *Antropologia kultury* [*Anthropology of Culture*]. Wydawnictwo Zysk i Spółka, Warszawa.

Burszta W.J. (2004). Tolerancja w dyskursie zagranicznym [Tolerance in international discourse]. In A. Posern-Zieliński [ed.] *Tolerancja i jej granice w relacjach międzykulturowych* [*Tolerance and its Limits in Intercultural Relations*]. Wydawnictwo Poznańskie, Poznań.

Buzan B. (2004). *From International to World Society?* Cambridge University Press, Cambridge.

Bystroń J.S. (1995). *Megalomania narodowa* [*National Megalomania*]. Wydawnictwo Wiedza i Książka, Warszawa.

Cammaerts B. (2015). Technologies of self-mediation: Affordances and constraints of social media form protest movements. In J. Uldam, A. Vestergaard [eds.] *Civic Engagement and Social Media*. Palsgrave Macmillan, London.

Casmir F. (1996). Budowanie trzeciej kultury: zmiana paradygmatu [Third-culture building: A paradigm shift]. In A. Kapciak, L. Korporowicz, A. Tyszka [eds.] *Komunikacja międzykulturowa* [*Intercultural Communication*]. Instytut Kultury, Warszawa.

Castells M. (2007). Communication, Power and Counter-power in the Network Society. *International Journal of Communication*, 1, 238–266.

Castells M. (2009). *Siła tożsamości* [*The Power of Identity*]. Wydawnictwo Naukowe PWN, Warszawa.

Castells M. (2013). *Władza komunikacji* [*Communication Power*]. Wydawnictwo Naukowe PWN, Warszawa.

Castles S., Miller M.J. (2011). *Migracje we współczesnym świecie* [*The Age of Migration*]. Wydawnictwo Naukowe PWN, Warszawa.

Castles S., de Haas H., Miller M.J. (2014). *The Age of Migration: International Population Movements in the Modern World*, Fifth Edition. Palgrave Macmillan, London.

Chaiken S. (1987). The Heuristic Model of Persuasion. *Social Influence*, 5, 3–39.

Chen G.M. (2012). The Impact of New Media on Intercultural Communication in Global context. *China Media Research*, 8(2), 1–10.

Davis A. (2007). *Public Relations*. Polskie Wydawnictwo Ekonomiczne, Warszawa.

Dombrowsky D. (2012). Constructing Identity on Social Networks: An analysis of Competences of Communication Constructed on Facebook.com. *Central European Journal of Communication*, 1(8), 91–103.

Dörner A. (2006). *Politik als Fiktion*. Aus der Politik und Zeitgeschichte, 7, 3–11.

Dyła M. (2011). New media – The new society? In K. Kopecka-Piech, A. Woźny [eds.] *New Media Studies*. Wydawnictwo Uniwersytetu Wrocławskiego, Wrocław.

Edwards G. (2014). *Social Movements and Protest*. Cambridge University Press, Cambridge.

Friedman T.L. (2001). *Lexus i drzewo oliwne* [*The Lexus and the Olive Tree*]. Dom Wydawniczy Rebis, Poznań.

Friedman T.L. (2006). *Świat jest płaski: Krótka historia XXI wieku* [*The World is Flat: A Brief History of the Twenty-first Century*]. Dom Wydawniczy Rebis, Poznań.

Fukuyama F. (2005). *Koniec człowieka: Konsekwencje rewolucji biotechnologicznej* [*Our Posthuman Future: Consequences of the Biotechnology Revolution*]. Wydawnictwo Znak, Kraków.

Galtung J., Holmboe Ruge M. (1965). The Structure of Foreign News: The Presentation of the Congo, Cuba and Cyprus Crisis in Four Norwegian Newspapers. *Journal of Peace Research*, 2, 64–91.

Garland C. (2015). As barriers fall, contingency becomes possibility. In I.R. Lamond, K. Spracklen [eds.] *Protests as Events. Politics, Activism and Leisure*. Rowman & Littlefield, London.

Geertz C. (1966). The Impact of the Concept of Culture on the Concept of Man. *Journal Bulletin of the Atomic Scientists*, 22(4), 2–8.

Gellner E. (2009). *Narody i nacjonalizm* [*Nations and Nationalism*]. Wydawnictwo Difin, Warszawa.

Gesteland R.R. (2000). *Różnice kulturowe a zachowania w biznesie. Marketing, negocjacje i zarządzanie w różnych kulturach* [*Cross-cultural Business Behaviour. Marketing, Negotiating, and Managing Across Cultures*]. Wydawnictwo Naukowe PWN, Warszawa.

Goffman E. (2000). Człowiek w teatrze życia codziennego, [The Presentation of Self in Everyday Life]. Wydawnictwo KR, Warszawa.

Golebiowska E.A. (2014). *The Many Faces of Tolerance: Attitudes towards Diversity in Poland*. Routledge, New York.

Gorman L., McLean D. (2009). *Media i społeczeństwo. Wprowadzenie historyczne* [*Media and Society. A Historical Introduction*]. Wydawnictwo Uniwersytetu Jagiellońskiego, Kraków.

Gudykunst W., Chua E., Gray A. (1987). Cultural Dissimilarities and Uncertainty Reduction Processes. In M. McLaughlin [ed.] *Communication Yearbook*, 10, Sage, Newbury Park, CA, 456–469.

Gudykunst W.B., Young Y.K. (2003). *Communication with Strangers. An Approach to Intercultural Communication*. McGraw-Hill, New York.

Guinier L., Torres G. (2002). *Miners Canary: Enlisting Race Resisting Power, Transforming Democracy*. Harvard University Press, Cambridge.

Hall E.T. (1984). *Poza kulturą* [*Beyond Culture*]. Państwowe Wydawnictwo Naukowe, Warszawa.

Hall S. (1987). Kodowanie i dekodowanie [Encoding/Decoding]. *Przekazy i opinie*, 1–2, 58–71.

Hampden-Turner C., Trompenaars A. (2006). *Siedem kultur kapitalizmu* [*The Seven Cultures of Capitalism*]. Oficyna Ekonomiczna, Kraków.

Hochschild A.R. (2009). *Zarządzanie emocjami: Komercjalizacja ludzkich uczuć* [*The Managed Heart: Commercialization of Human Feeling*]. Wydawnictwo Naukowe PWN, Warszawa.

Hofstede G., Hofstede G.J. (2007). *Kultury i organizacje* [*Cultures and Organizations*]. Polskie Wydawnictwo Ekonomiczne, Warszawa.

Huntington S.P. (1996). *Zderzenie cywilizacji* [*Clash of Civilizations*]. Warszawskie Wydawnictwo Literackie Muza SA, Warszawa.

Husband, C., Alam Y. (2011). Social Cohesion and Counter Terrorism. Policy Press, Bristol.

Joppke Ch. (2004). The Retreat of Multiculturalism in the Liberal State: Theory and Policy. *The British Journal of Sociology*, 55(2): 237–257.

Keen A. (2007). *Kult amatora. Jak internet niszczy kulturę* [*The Cult of the Amateur: How Today's Internet is Killing Our Culture*]. Wydawnictwa Akademickie i Profesjonalne, Warszawa.

Kemmis S., McTaggart R. (2010). Uczestniczące badanie interwencyjne. Działanie komunikacyjne i sfera publiczna [Participatory action research: Communicative action and the public sphere]. In N.K. Denzin, Y.S. Lincoln [eds.] *Metody badań jakościowych* [*Qualitative Research Methods*]. T. 1. Wydawnictwo Naukowe PWN, Warszawa.

King S.W. (1975). *Communication and Social Influence*. Addison-Wesley Publishing Company, Boston.

King J.E. (1995). Culture centered knowledge: Black studies, curriculum transformations and social action. In J.A. Banks, C.M. Banks [eds.] *Handbook of Research on Multicultural Education*. Macmillan, New York.

Kosowska E. (2007). Przestrzenie tożsamości [Spaces of identity]. In W. Kalaga [ed.] *Dylematy wielokulturowości* [*The Dilemmas of Multiculturalism*]. Wydawnictwo Universitas, Kraków.

Kotowicz D. (2006). Internet – szanse i zagrożenia dla demokracji [Internet – Opportunities and threats to democracy]. In D. Batorski, M. Marody, A. Nowak [eds.] *Społeczna przestrzeń Internetu* [*Social Space of the Internet*]. Wydawnictwo SWPS Academica, Warszawa.

Kozłowska A. (2006). *Oddziaływanie mass mediów* [*Influence of Mass Media*]. Oficyna Wydawnicza SGH, Warszawa.

Kraszewski P. (2003). Typologia migracji [Typology of migration]. In J. Burszta, J. Serwański [eds.] *Migracja – Europa – Polska* [*Migration – Europe – Poland*]. Zakład Badań Narodowościowych PAN, Poznań.

Kuczyńska A. (2014). Social media a działania obywatelskie [Social media and civic action]. In M. Jezierski, A. Seklecka, Ł. Wojtkowski [eds.] Nowe media. *Między dziennikarstwem obywatelskim a polityką* [*New Media. Between Civic Journalism and Politics*]. Wydawnictwo Naukowe UMK, Toruń.

Kuligowski W., Pomieciński A. (2010). Dlaczego globalne zawsze jest lokalne? [Why is global always local?]. In W. Kuligowski, A. Pomieciński [eds.] *Różne kultury, różne globalizacje* [*Different Cultures, Different Globalisations*]. Wydawnictwo Poznańskie, Poznań.

Kunce A. (2007). Zlokalizować tożsamość [Locate the identity]. In W. Kalaga [ed.] *Dylematy wielokulturowości* [*The Dilemmas of Multiculturalism*]. Wydawnictwo Universitas, Kraków.

Kunczik M., Zipfel A. (2000). *Wprowadzenie do nauki o dziennikarstwie i komunikowaniu* [*Introduction to Journalism and Communication*]. Wydawnictwo Scholar, Warszawa.

Kundnani A. (2007). Integrationism: The Politics of Anti-Muslim Racism. *Race&Class* 48(4), 24–44.

Kymlicka W. (1996). *Multicultural Citizenship. A Liberal Theory of Minority Rights*. Clarendon Press, Oxford.

Kymlicka W. (1998). Ethic relations and western political theory. In M. Opalski [ed.] *Managing Diversity in Plural Societies. Minorities, Migration and Nation-Building in Post-Communist Europe*. Forum Eastern Europe, Ottawa.

Kymlicka W. (2003). *New forms of citizenship*. In T.J. Courchesne, D.J. Savoie [eds.] *The Art of the State. Governance in a World without Frontiers*. IRPP, Montreal.

Ladson-Billings G., Donnor J. (2010). Krytyczna teoria rasy i jej znaczenie etyczne [Critical race theory and its ethical significance]. In N.K. Denzin, Y.S. Lincoln [eds.] *Metody badań jakościowych* [*Qualitative Research Methods*]. T. 1. Wydawnictwo PWN, Warszawa.

Levi-Strauss C. (1960). *Smutek tropików* [*A World on the Wane*]. Państwowy Instytut Wydawniczy, Warszawa.

Lievrouw L.A. (2012). *Media alternatywne i zaangażowanie społeczne* [*Alternative and Activist New Media*]. Wydawnictwo Naukowe PWN, Warszawa.

Lister, M., Dovey, J., Giddings, S., Grant, J., Kelly, K. (2004). New media: A Critical Introduction. Routledge, London.

Łodziński S. (2003). Globalizacja a instytucja "obywatelstwa narodowego". Wokół dyskusji na temat zasad nadawania obywatelstwa imigrantom z krajów pozaeuropejskich w Unii Europejskiej [Globalisation and "National Citizenship"]. In J. Zdanowski [ed.] *Globalizacja a tożsamość* [*Globalisation and Identity*]. Wydawnictwo Naukowe Askon, Warszawa.

Łukowski W. (2008). Współczesne migracje – potencjał konsensu politycznego? [Contemporary migration – Potential of political consensus?]. In G. Firlit-Fesnak [ed.] *Migracje międzynarodowe a modernizacja systemu politycznego i społecznego* [*International Migration and Modernisation of the Political and Social System*]. Oficyna Wydawnicza Aspra-JR, Warszawa.

Lustig M.W., Koester J. (2003). *Intercultural Competence*. Allyn and Bacon, Boston.

Maffesoli M. (2008). *Czas plemion* [*The Time of the Tribes*]. Wydawnictwo Naukowe PWN, Warszawa.

Mamzer H. (2003). *Tożsamość w podróży. Wielokulturowość a kształtowanie tożsamości jednostki* [*Identity in Travelling. Multiculturality and Formation of an Individual Identity*]. Wydawnictwo Uniwersytetu Adama Mickiewicza, Poznań.

Mathews G. (2000). *Supermarket kultury* [*Cultural Supermarket*]. Państwowy Instytut Wydawniczy, Warszawa.

McLaren P. (1994). White terror and oppositional agency: towards critical multiculturalism. In D.T. Goldberg [ed.] *Multiculturalism: A Critical Reader*. Blackwell, Oxford.

McLuhan M. (2004). *Zrozumieć media: Przedłużenia człowieka* [*Understanding Media: The Extensions of Man*]. Wydawnictwa Naukowo-Techniczne, Warszawa.

McQuail D. (2000). *Mass Communication Theory*. Sage, London.

Michalczyk S. (2013). Teoria wartości informacji historia i współczesność [News value theory: History and the present]. *Studia Politicae Universitatis Silesiensis*, 10, 131–146.

Mikułowski Pomorski J. (2003). *Komunikacja międzykulturowa* [*Intercultural Communication*]. Wydawnictwo Akademii Ekonomicznej w Krakowie, Kraków.

Mikułowski Pomorski J. (2007a). *Jak narody porozumiewają się ze sobą w komunikacji międzykulturowej i komunikowaniu medialnym* [*How Nations Communicate: Intercultural Communication and the Media*]. Wydawnictwo Universitas, Kraków.

Mikułowski Pomorski J. (2007b). Współczesny problem kulturowości i wielokulturowości w komunikowaniu [Contemporary problem of culturalism and multiculturalism in communication]. In M. Ratajczak [ed.] *Multikulturalizm w sferze mediów* [*Multiculturalism in the Media*]. Wydawnictwo Uniwersytetu Wrocławskiego, Wrocław.

Modood T. (2014). *Multikulturalizm* [*Multiculturalism*]. Wydawnictwo Nauka i Innowacje, Poznań.

Molenda-Zdziech M. (2001). Socjologiczna problematyka komunikowania masowego [Sociological problems of mass communication]. In B. Jung [ed.] *Media, komunikacja, biznes elektroniczny* [*Media, Communication, Electronic Business*]. Wydawnictwo Difin, Warszawa.

Możejko E. (2007). Wielka szansa czy iluzja: wielokulturowość w dobie ponowoczesności [Big chance or illusion: Multiculturalism in the postmodern era]. In W. Kalaga [ed.] *Dylematy wielokulturowości* [*The Dilemmas of Multiculturalism*]. Wydawnictwo Universitas, Kraków.

Mrozek-Dumanowska A. (2003). Konstrukcja światów symbolicznych jako alternatywa globalizacji [Construction of symbolic worlds as an alternative to globalisation]. In J. Zdanowski [ed.] *Globalizacja a tożsamość* [*Globalisation and Identity*]. Wydawnictwo Naukowe Askon, Warszawa.

Mrozowski M. (1991). *Między manipulacją a poznaniem. Człowiek w świecie mass mediów* [*Between Manipulation and Cognition. The Man in the World of Mass Media*]. Centralny Ośrodek Metodyki Upowszechniania Kultury, Warszawa.

Mrozowski M. (2001). *Media masowe. Władza, rozrywka i biznes* [*Mass media. Power, Entertainment and Business*]. ASPRA-JR, Warszawa.

Niedźwiedzki D. (2010). *Migracje i tożsamość. Od teorii do analizy przypadku* [*Migration and Identity. From Theory to Case Analysis*]. Zakład Wydawniczy NOMOS, Kraków.

Nikitorowicz J. (2000). Socjotechnika w edukacji regionalnej i międzykulturowej wobec celów i wartości młodzieży oraz idei zjednoczenia Europy [Social engineering in regional and intercultural education in the face of objectives and values of youth and the idea of European unity]. In T. Lewowicki, E. Ogrodzka-Mazur, A. Szczurek-Boruta [eds.] *Edukacja międzykulturowa w Polsce i na świecie* [*Intercultural Education in Poland and in the World*]. Wydawnictwo Uniwersytetu Śląskiego, Katowice.

Nikitorowicz J. (2012). Nowe wyzwania edukacji międzykulturowej w kontekście współczesnych dylematów wokół kreowania społeczeństwa wielokulturowego [New challenges of intercultural education in the context of contemporary dilemmas around creating a multicultural society]. In M. Biernacka, K. Krzysztofiak, A. Sadowski [eds.] *Społeczeństwo wielokulturowe – nowe szanse i zagrożenia* [*Multicultural Society – New Opportunities and Threats*]. Wydawnictwo Uniwersytetu w Białymstoku, Białystok.

Nowicki J. (2001). L'homme des confins: pour une anthropologie interculturelle. In D. Bougnoux, Y. Jeanneret [eds.] *Emergence et continuité dans les recherches en information et communication*. SFSIC, Paris, 95–104.

Okólski M. (2006). *Demografia. Podstawowe pojęcia, procesy, i teorie w encyklopedycznym zarysie* [*Demography. Basic Concepts, Processes and Theories – An Encyclopaedic Outline*]. Wydawnictwo Naukowe Scholar, Warszawa.

O'Reilly K. (2012). *International Migration & Social Theory*. Palsgrave Macmillan, Hampshire.

Paleczny T. (2005). *Stosunki międzykulturowe. Zarys problematyki* [*Intercultural Relations. An Outline*]. Krakowskie Towarzystwo Edukacyjne, Kraków.

Paleczny T. (2006). Stosunki międzykulturowe: Modele pluralizmu w społeczeństwach "ponowoczesnych" [Intercultural relations: Models of pluralism in "postmodern" Societies]. In K. Golemo, T. Paleczny, E. Wiącek [eds.] *Wzory wielokulturowości we współczesnym świecie* [*Patterns of Multiculturalism in Contemporary World*]. Wydawnictwo Uniwersytetu Jagiellońskiego, Kraków.

Paleczny T. (2007). *Interpersonalne stosunku międzykulturowe* [*Interpersonal International Relations*]. Wydawnictwo Uniwersytetu Jagiellońskiego, Kraków.

Paleczny T. (2008). *Socjologia tożsamości* [*Sociology of Identity*]. Krakowskie Towarzystwo Edukacyjne, Kraków.

Pettigrew T.F. (1998). Reactions toward the New Minorities of Western Europe. *Annual Review of Sociology*, 24, 77–103.

Piechota G., Rajczyk R. (2015). The Role of Social Media during Protests on Maidan. *Communication Today*, 6(2), 86–97.

Podrez E. (2004). Tolerancja – problemy i dylematy nie tylko moralnej natury [Tolerance – Problems and dilemmas of not only moral nature]. In A. Borowiak, P. Szarota [eds.] *Tolerancja i wielokulturowość. Wyzwania XXI wieku* [*Tolerance and Multiculturalism. Challenges of the 21st Century*]. Wydawnictwo SWPS Academica, Warszawa.

Portes A., Borocz J. (2010). Contemporary immigration. Theoretical perspectives on its determinants and modes of incorporation. In S. Vertovec [ed.] *Migration*. Routledge, London and New York.

Posern-Zieliński A. (2004). Negocjowanie tolerancji, czyli między groźbą a dążeniem do współdziałania [Negotiating tolerance – Between a threat and trying to cooperate]. In A. Posern-Zieliński [ed.] *Tolerancja i jej granice w relacjach międzykulturowych* [*Tolerance and Its Limits in Intercultural Relations*]. Wydawnictwo Poznańskie, Poznań.

Rajczyk R. (2016). *Nowoczesne wojny informacyjne* [*Modern Information Wars*]. Wydawnictwo Difin, Warszawa.

Ratajczak M. (2004). *Jak porozumiewają się Szwajcarzy. Media w wielokulturowej Szwajcarii* [*How the Swiss Communicate. Media in Intercultural Switzerland*]. Wydawnictwo Uniwersytetu Wrocławskiego, Wrocław.

Ratajczak M. (2006). Komunikacja międzykulturowa – wybrane zagadnienia [Intercultural communication – Selected issues]. In M. Ratajczak [ed.] *Pomiędzy kulturami. szkice z komunikacji międzykulturowej* [*Between Cultures. Outline of Intercultural Communication*]. Wydawnictwo Uniwersytetu Wrocławskiego, Wrocław.

Ratajczak Z. (2000). Wprowadzenie [Introduction]. In Z. Ratajczak [ed.] *Wpływ społeczny. Badania i praktyka* [*Social Impact. Studies and Practice*]. T. 8. Kolokwia Psychologiczne (Psychological Colloquia), Warszawa.

Romaniszyn K. (2003). *Kulturowe Implikacje Międzynarodowych Migracji* [*Cultural Implications of International Migration*]. Wydawnictwo Katolickiego Uniwersytetu Lubelskiego, Lublin.

Rosenau J.N. (1969). *Public Opinion and Foreign Policy*. Random House, New York.

Ryniejska-Kiełdanowicz M. (2011). Kulturowe aspekty działań public relations [Cultural aspects of public relations activities]. In G. Piechota [ed.] *Public Relations. Konteksty międzykulturowe i międzynarodowe* [*Public Relations. Intercultural and International Contexts*]. Oficyna Wydawnicza AFM, Kraków.

Samovar L., Porter R. (1994). An introduction to intercultural communication. In L. Samovar, R. Porter [eds.] *Intercultural Communication*. Wadsworth, California.

Schnapper D. (1991). A Host Country of Immigrants That Does Know Itself. *Diaspora* 1(3), 353–363.

Schow M. (1994). *Global Society and International Relations*. Cambridge University Press, Cambridge.

Schwartz S.H., Verkasalo M., Antonosky A. (1997). Value Priorities and Social Desirability: Much Substance, Some Style. *British Journal of Social Psychology*, 36, 3–18.

Skarżyńska K. (2009). Czy media elektroniczne tworzą sztuczny świat? Rola mediów elektronicznych w rozumieniu świata i kształtowaniu postaw [Do electronic media create an artificial world? The role of electronic media in understanding the world and shaping attitudes]. In M. Filiciak, G. Ptaszek [eds.] *Komunikowanie (się) w mediach elektronicznych. Język, edukacja, semiotyka* [*Communicating in Electronic Media. Language, Education, Semiotics*]. Wydawnictwa Akademickie i Profesjonalne, Warszawa.

Skarżyńska K., Henne K. (2007). *Szkoła, media, kapitał społeczny, szczęście* [*School, Media, Social Capital, Happiness*]. Kolokwia Psychologiczne (Psychological Colloquia), 13, 65–93.

Soja M., Zborowski A. (2011). Wymiar etniczny struktury społecznej Krakowa – przeszłość i czasy współczesne [Ethnic Dimension of Krakow's Social Structure – The Past and the Present]. *Peregrinus Cracoviensis*, 22, 217–232.

Soysal Y.N. (1994). *Limits of Citizenship. Migrants and Postnational Membership in Europe*. University of Chicago Press, Chicago.

Stephan W.G., Stephan C.W. (2003). *Wywieranie wpływu przez grupy* [*Intergroup Relations*]. Gdańskie Wydawnictwo Psychologiczne, Gdańsk.

Svensson B. (2008). Kulturowe granice obywatelstwa [Cultural limits of citizenship]. In E.H. Oleksy [ed.] *Tożsamość i obywatelstwo w społeczeństwie wielokulturowym* [*Identity and Citizenship in Multicultural Society*]. Wydawnictwo Naukowe PWN, Warszawa.

Szacka B. (2003). *Wprowadzenie do socjologii* [*Introduction to Sociology*]. Oficyna Naukowa, Warszawa.

Szahaj A. (2004). *E Pluribus Unum? Dylematy wielokulturowości i politycznej poprawności* [*Dilemmas of Multiculturalism and Political Correctness*]. Wydawnictwo Universitas, Kraków.

Szopski M. (2005). *Komunikowanie międzykulturowe* [*Intercultural Communication*]. Wydawnictwa Szkolne i Pedagogiczne, Warszawa.

Sztompka P. (2007). *Socjologia* [*Sociology*]. Wydawnictwo Znak, Kraków.

Szymczak W. (2007). Znaczenie wartości w tworzeniu społeczeństwa obywatelskiego [Significance of values in creating civil society]. In E. Balawajder [ed.] *Społeczeństwo obywatelskie* [*Civil Society*]. Wydawnictwo Katolickiego Uniwersytetu Lubelskiego, Lublin.

Taylor C. (1994). *Multiculturalism. Examining the Politics of Recognition.* Princeton University Press, Princeton.

Taylor C. (1995). Źródła współczesnej tożsamości [Sources of modern identity]. In K. Michalski [ed.] *Europa i społeczeństwo obywatelskie. Rozmowy w Castel Gandolfo* [*Europe and Civil Society. Conversations in Castel Gandolfo*]. Społeczny Instytut Wydawniczy Znak, Kraków.

Tilly C. (2008). *Demokracja* [*Democracy*]. Wydawnictwo Naukowe PWN, Warszawa.

Ting-Toomey S. (1999). *Communication across Cultures.* Guilford Press, New York.

Trąbka A. (2014). *Tożsamość rekonstruowana. Znaczenie migracji w biografiach. Third Culture Kids* [*Reconstructed Identity. Significance of Migration in Biographies. Third Culture Kids*]. Wydawnictwo Naukowe Scholar, Warszawa.

van Dijk J. (2010). *Społeczne aspekty nowych mediów* [*The Network Society: Social Aspects of New Media*]. Wydawnictwo Naukowe PWN, Warszawa.

van Dijk T. (2000). New(s)rasism. A discourse analytical approach. In S. Cottle [ed.] *Ethnic Minorities and the Media.* Open University Press, Buckingham.

Vinuales, G. (2011). Impact of Cultural Values in Social Network Sites: The Case of Facebook. *China Media Research*, 8(2), 1–10.

Warat M. (2008). Obywatelstwo wielokulturowe – projekt teoretyczny czy europejska codzienność? [Multicultural citizenship – A theoretical project or European daily reality?]. In A. Kościański, W. Misztal [eds.] *Społeczeństwo obywatelskie. Między ideą a praktyką* [*Civil Society. Between the Idea and Practice*]. Wydawnictwo Instytutu Filozofii i Socjologii PAN, Warszawa.

Welsch W. (1998). Transkulturowość. Nowa koncepcja kultury [Transculturalism. A new cultural concept]. In R. Kubicki [ed.] *Filozoficzne konteksty rozumu transwersalnego* [*Philosophical Contexts of Transversal Mind*]. Wydawnictwo Fundacja Humaniora, Poznań.

West R.L., Turner L.H. (2013). *Introducing Communication Theory: Analysis and Application.* McGraw-Hill, New York.

Wnuk-Lipiński E. (2004). *Świat międzyepoki. Globalizacja, demokracja, państwo narodowe* [*The Inter-era World. Globalisation, Democracy, Nation State*]. Wydawnictwo Znak, Kraków.

Wódz K. (2007). *Negocjowana demokracja, czyli europejskie governance po polsku* [*Negotiated Democracy, or European Governance, the Polish Way*]. Wydawnictwo Naukowe Scholar, Warszawa.

Wódz K., Niesporek A. (2008). Negocjowana demokracja, czyli europejskie governance po polsku [Negotiated democracy, or European governance, the Polish way]. In A. Kościański, W. Misztal [eds.] *Społeczeństwo obywatelskie. Między ideą a praktyką* [*Civil Society. Between Idea and Practice*]. Wydawnictwo Instytutu Filozofii i Socjologii PAN, Warszawa.

Wódz K., Wódz J. (2007). Europa urzędników brukselskich czy Europa obywateli? U źródeł deficytu demokratycznego w Unii Europejskiej [Europe of union officials or Europe of citizens. At the source of democratic deficit in the European Union]. In K. Wódz [ed.] *Negocjowana demokracja, czyli europejskie governance po polsku* [*Negotiated Democracy, or European Governance, the Polish Way*]. Wydawnictwo Naukowe Scholar, Warszawa.

Zacher L. (2003). *Spór o globalizację* [*Controversy over Globalisation*]. Dom Wydawniczy Elipsa, Warszawa.

Zientara P. (2012). *Międzynarodowe migracje o charakterze ekonomicznym: przyczyny, mechanizmy, konsekwencje* [*International Economic Migrations: Causes, Mechanisms, Consequences*]. Wydawnictwo Uniwersytetu Gdańskiego, Gdańsk.

## Electronic references

Applebaum A. (2015). *Mark Zuckerberg Should Spend $45 Billion on Undoing Facebook's Damage to Democracies*. https://www.washingtonpost.com/opinions/mark-zuckerberg-could-spend-45-billion-on-undoing-facebooks-damage/2015/12/10/4b7d1ba0-9e91-11e5-a3c5-c77f2cc5a43c_story.html?utm_term=.d31971653558 – accessed on 11.01.2017.

Kaznowski D. (2010). *Podział i klasyfikacja social media* [*Division and Classification of Social Media*]. http://networkeddigital.com/2010/05/10/podzial-i-klasyfikacja-social-media/ – accessed on 15.11.2016.

Mazurczak G. (2009). Międzykulturowość w zglobalizowanym świecie [Interculturalism in a Globalised World]. Portal Spraw Zagranicznych. http://www.psz.pl/124-polityka/grzegorz-mazurczak-miedzykulturowo sc-w-zglobalizowanym-swiecie – accessed on 15.11.2016.

Piechota G. (2014). The Role of Social Media in Creating Intercultural Dialogue and Overcoming Prejudice – A Comparative Analysis of Pilot Survey Results. *KOME – An International Journal of Pure Communication Inquiry*, 2(2), 37–63. http://komejournal.com/files/Piechota%20 KOME.pdf – accessed on 4.01.2017.

Ratajczak M. (2014). *Nowe media – nowe tożsamości?* [*New Media – New Identities?*]. http://www.kulturaihistoria.umcs.lublin.pl/archives/5003 – accessed on 11.01.2017.

Sawyer R. (2011). *The Impact of New Social Media on Intercultural Adaptation*. http://digitalcommons.uri.edu/srhonorsprog/242 – accessed on 2.02.2017.

Veltri, N.F., Elgarah, W. (2009). The Role of National Cultural Differences in User Adoption of Social Networking. *SAIS 2009 Proceedings*. http://www.academia.edu/1201671/The_role_of_national_cultural_differences_in_user_adoption_of_social_networking – accessed on 2.02.2017.

Zawilska-Florczuk M., Ciechanowicz A. (2011). *Jeden kraj, dwa społeczeństwa? Niemcy 20 lat po zjednoczeniu* [*One Country, Two Societies? Germany 20 years after Reunification*]. https://www.osw.waw.pl/sites/default/files/prace_35_0.pdf – accessed on 23.05.2017.

# List of Tables and Charts



## List of charts

# Index of Names

# Index of Subjects

www.ingramcontent.com/pod-product-compliance
Ingram Content Group UK Ltd.
Pitfield, Milton Keynes, MK11 3LW, UK
UKHW021833100926
8556IPUK00004B/312

9 783631 748626